CONSTRUCTIONS

An Experimental Approach to Intensely Local Architectures

ARCHITECTURAL DESIGN
March/April 2015
Profile No 234

Guest-Edited by MICHAEL HENSEL
AND CHRISTIAN HERMANSEN CORDUA

ISSN 0003-8504
ISBN 978-1118-700570

Editorial Offices
John Wiley & Sons
25 John Street
London WC1N 2BS
UK

T +44 (0)20 8326 3800

Editor
Helen Castle

Managing Editor (Freelance)
Caroline Ellerby

Production Editor
Elizabeth Gongde

Prepress
Artmedia, London

Art Direction + Design
CHK Design:
Christian Küsters
Sophie Troppmair

Printed in Italy by Printer
Trento Srl

Cover: Scarcity and
Creativity Studio, 2x2
Bathing Platform, Nusfjord,
Norway, 2012. © Michael
Hensel/Scarcity and
Creativity Studio, 2012

Inside cover: Scarcity and
Creativity Studio (SCL),
Floating Compression
Canopy, Nusfjord, Lofoten,
Norway, 2013. © Michael
Hensel, Scarcity and
Creativity Studio

02/2015

⅄Ⅾ ARCHITECTURAL DESIGN

March/April
2015

Profile No.
234

Journal Customer Services
For ordering information,
claims and any enquiry
concerning your journal
subscription please go to
www.wileycustomerhelp
.com/ask or contact your
nearest office.

Americas
E: cs-journals@wiley.com
T: +1 781 388 8598 or
+1 800 835 6770 (toll free
in the USA & Canada)

**Europe, Middle East
and Africa**
E: cs-journals@wiley.com
T: +44 (0) 1865 778315

Asia Pacific
E: cs-journals@wiley.com
T: +65 6511 8000

Japan (For Japanese
speaking support)
E: cs-japan@wiley.com
T: +65 6511 8010 or 005 316
50 480 (toll-free)

Visit our Online Customer
Help available in 7 languages
at www.wileycustomerhelp
.com/ask

Print ISSN: 0003-8504
Online ISSN: 1554-2769

Prices are for six issues
and include postage and
handling charges. Individual-
rate subscriptions must be
paid by personal cheque or
credit card. Individual-rate
subscriptions may not be
resold or used as library
copies.

All prices are subject to
change without notice.

Identification Statement
Periodicals Postage paid
at Rahway, NJ 07065.
Air freight and mailing in
the USA by Mercury Media
Processing, 1850 Elizabeth
Avenue, Suite C, Rahway,
NJ 07065, USA.

USA Postmaster
Please send address changes
to *Architectural Design*, c/o
Mercury Media Processing,
1634 E. Elizabeth Avenue,
Linden, NJ 07036, USA.

Subscribe to ⅄Ⅾ
⅄Ⅾ is published bimonthly
and is available to purchase
on both a subscription basis
and as individual volumes
at the following prices.

Prices
Individual copies:
£24.99 / US$39.95
Individual issues on
⅄Ⅾ App for iPad:
£9.99 / US$13.99
Mailing fees for print
may apply

Annual Subscription Rates
Student: £75 / US$117
print only
Personal: £120 / US$189
print and iPad access
Institutional: £212 / US$398
print or online
Institutional: £244 / US$457
combined print and online
6-issue subscription on
⅄Ⅾ App for iPad: £44.99 /
US$64.99

MIX
Paper from
responsible sources
FSC® C015829
www.fsc.org

In the last decade, there has been a seismic shift in architecture. Whereas once architectural design centred, with very few exceptions, on drawing, design and representation, in the last decade making has become the main motor of innovation. Within the pages of △, this has manifested itself in issues such as *Design through Making* (July/August 2005) and *Protoarchitecture: Analogue and Digital Hybrids* (July/August 2008) guest-edited by Bob Sheil; *Made by Robots: Challenging Architecture at a Larger Scale* (May/June 2014) guest-edited by Fabio Gramazio and Matthias Kohler; and the forthcoming *Pavilions, Pop-ups and Parasols: The Impact of Social Media on Physical Space* (May/June 2015), guest-edited by Leon van Schaik and Fleur Watson. In schools internationally, this transference in emphasis towards fabrication has culminated in investment in large-scale workshops and machinery. Guest-Editors Michael Hensel and Christian Hermansen Cordua articulate clearly in their introduction how pivotal making has become a force for innovation, investigation and learning in architecture: 'The issue seeks to foreground the notion of "construction" because the schools and practices portrayed in this issue define their stance – perhaps even "research their positions" – through actual building. Building is, then, not just the implementation of represented conceptions, but rather seen as a process by which one discovers and explores.'

What differentiates this △ title from other publications on making is its emphasis on localness. For the guest-editors, a locally specific architecture provides a significant 'antidote to unchecked globalisation' and 'homogenisation'. Rather than prescribing a one-stock formal response or regional style, Hensel and Hermansen Cordua espouse a plurality of design solutions, as reflected in the diversity of contributions that are drawn from across continents: from Norway and Spain to Chile, Alabama and New York to India. Structures respond to distinct local conditions through a performative approach; the emphasis lies not in individual creativity or formal impact, but on interpreting data from local site and climatic conditions to best inform design decisions, often marrying up current technology with a local tectonic sensibility. As a project, *Constructions* with its emphasis on experimentation and localness remains a fecund work in progress, as suggested by the guest-editors' concluding article, 'Outlook: En Route to Intensely Local Architectures and Tectonics', in which they sum up and provide some pointers for further research. For the Counterpoint for this issue, author and sustainability expert Terri Peters was asked to step into this gap and explore further the sustainable potential for this type of work, highlighting how place-based projects, informed by a sense of locality, might from a sustainable point of view also help to privilege the quality of human experience. △

Michael Hensel

Performance-Oriented
Architecture: Rethinking
Architecture and the Built
Environment

2013

Michael Hensel and Jeffrey
P Turko

Grounds and Envelopes:
Reshaping Architecture and the
Built Environment

2015

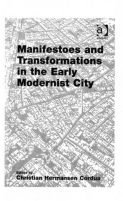

top left and centre: The covers of Hensel's
latest books that explore themes and
examine projects en route to locally specific
architectures.

Christian Hermansen Cordua

Manifestoes and
Transformations in the
Early Modernist City

2010

top right: Cover of Hermansen Cordua's
edited book on Modernist conceptions
of the city and large-scale urban
transformations.

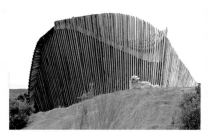

Christian Hermansen Cordua

Hospedería de las Alas,
Open City, Ritoque, Chile

2012

2x2 Bathing Platform,
Nusfjord, Lofoten, Norway

2013

Community Centre, Pumanque,
Chile

2014

centre (all): Various projects utilising screen
walls and surfaces. The projects illustrate
Hermansen Cordua's interest in screen wall-
like surfaces that provide transitional spaces
and reduce climatic impact on interior
spaces.

Michael Hensel and Defne
Sunguroğlu Hensel

Membrane Spaces Workshop

Izmir University of Economics

Izmir, Turkey

2009

bottom: The studies of arrayed membrane
systems illustrate Michael Hensel's
interest in textile auxiliary architectures.

Michael Hensel is an architect, researcher, writer and tenured professor at the Oslo School of Architecture and Design (AHO) where he directs the Research Center for Architecture and Tectonics and co-directs the Scarcity and Creativity Studio (SCL). In his academic work he integrates research and education along a research-by-design trajectory with a strong emphasis on the development of non-discrete, performance-oriented and intensely local architectures, design-and-build efforts, and critical and projective capacities. He is a founding member of OCEAN and founding and current chairman of the OCEAN Design Research Association and the Sustainable Environment Association (SEA). He has authored and edited books and journals that relate to the themes pursued in this issue, most notably the △ Primer *Performance-Oriented Architecture: Rethinking Architectural Design and the Built Environment* (John Wiley & Sons, 2013) and, with Jeffrey P Turko, *Grounds and Envelopes: Reshaping Architecture and the Built Environment* (Routledge, 2015).

Christian Hermansen Cordua is an architect and tenured professor at AHO. He has studied and practised architecture in Chile, the US and the UK. From 1984 to 2002 he worked with both the Mackintosh School of Architecture at the Glasgow School of Art, where he was Director of Postgraduate Studies, and with Elder and Cannon Architects. In 2002 he moved to Oslo, where he was appointed Professor and Head of AHO's Institute of Architecture, a position he held until 2009. His most recent book is *Manifestoes and Transformations in the Early Modernist City* (Ashgate, 2010). He has contributed to journals, books and exhibitions in Europe and the US, and has recently held several European Union-funded research projects. During his career he has found the practice and teaching of architecture are a mutually enriching combination. The belief that architecture is only fully realised in buildings, along with an invitation to build at the Open City in Ritoque, Chile, made it possible to form the design/build Scarcity and Creativity Studio (SCL), which in turn motivated the research into the mode of didactic practice that is the origin of △ *Constructions.* ◠

INTRODUCTION

MICHAEL HENSEL AND
CHRISTIAN HERMANSEN CORDUA

Relating
Perceptions of
Constructions,
Experimental
and Local

Joakim Hoen, Seaside Second Home, south and west coast, Norway, 2012–

View of a locally specific design iteration of the system that underlies the project.

This title of ⌂ highlights two key notions of the proposed notion of 'constructions': the 'experimental' and the 'local'. While the experimental indicates the means by which projects might be conceived, the local constitutes the stated objective: the intensive search for contemporary locally specific architectures. The need for this arises from the ceaseless homogenisation of the built environment against a backdrop of global urbanisation, in which nondescript or generic architecture is all too often combined with individualism manifesting itself in highly idiosyncratic or 'sensational' designs; the upshot being a ubiquitous and indifferent mélange.

Architecture, like most spheres of life, is comprehensively affected by globalisation. This is borne out by the profusion and worldwide circulation of publications and online media that report on every major building; the fact that all large architecture firms engage in international practice; the worldwide standardisation of industrial building components and materials; and the standardisation of software as the dominant means to develop and represent architectural design. These are all factors that conspire against the possibility of developing an architecture that is first and foremost born out of distinct local conditions. This inevitably leads to an increasing homogeneity in urban form. Have we not all felt, with some disappointment, that after travelling long distances to a foreign city we could be 'anywhere' or 'everywhere' in terms of the character of the built environment? It is for this reason that this issue of ⚼ seeks to highlight directions taken by various schools and practices that could be seen as an antidote to unchecked globalisation.

The issue seeks to foreground the notion of 'construction' because the schools and practices that are portrayed define their stance – perhaps even 'research their positions' – through actual building. Building is, then, not just the implementation of represented conceptions, but rather seen as a process by which one discovers and explores. If construction is conceived as the mere implementation of a representation, any deviation from that representation becomes somewhat of an 'error'. In the case of the practices included in this issue of ⚼, an attitude can be detected in which construction is part of the process of conceiving architecture in an experimental manner. Experimentation allows design decisions to be made during the construction process. Another factor that aids experimentation in the case of the practices featured is that operating as small teams of often mixed expertise, and frequently dealing with unconventional clients, opens up possibilities not usually available in large institutional commissions.

We are of course not alone in sensing that architecture should move away from some of the excesses brought about by globalisation, as was implied by the 2014 Venice Architecture Biennale, entilted 'Fundamentals'. This exhibition, although not quite a 'radar' of changing sensibilities in architecture, may at least be seen as a 'seal of approval' of up and coming directions. The theme, which proposed an investigation into the basic constituents of buildings, which it called 'Elements', was a confirmation of a move away from 'signature' architecture and the 'star' architects who produce it, the memory of which

was shouted out through itheir total absence. That the individual exhibitions of each of the 'elements' displayed no more than a pedestrian catalogue of known facts and missed an opportunity to reinforce the theme of the Biennale as a whole does not take away from the perception of its curator, Rem Koolhaas, that the excesses of the last decades are, hopefully, coming to an end.

It is the notion of the 'local', then, that requires brief examination. This came forcefully to the fore in 1748 when the French political philosopher Charles-Louis de Secondat, Baron de Montesquieu (1689–1755) argued in his massively influential treatise 'The Spirit of the Laws' that locally specific environmental conditions – geography and climate – interact with local cultures and, in so doing, influence their inclination towards particular social arrangements and institutions. Montesquieu's understanding had considerable impact on the theory of the arts and architecture, where it was posited in similar terms that environmental conditions acted as particularising factors.[1] Gottfried Semper (1803–79), for instance, based his elaboration of the historical development of tectonics and stereotomics – and the associated crafts – precisely on the differences in local climate and available material conditions. More recently, Kenneth Frampton rearticulated this as 'two fundamental procedures: the tectonics of the frame, in which lightweight, linear components are assembled so as to encompass a spatial matrix, and the stereotomics of the earthwork, wherein mass and volume are conjointly formed through the repetitious piling up of heavy elements', and 'according to climate, custom, and available material the respective roles played by tectonics and stereotomics vary considerably'.[2] Modern architecture was frequently criticised for relinquishing local differences, although there exist numerous works that render such a comprehensive generalisation misconstrued. Nevertheless, this critical stance developed in the post-Second World War era into a distinct discourse that came to be known as regionalism. Alan Colquhoun has pointed out that regionalism from its origin in the

Walter Gropius, Masters' Houses, Dessau, Germany, 1929

top left: The pioneering designs for the Masters' Houses in Dessau constituted a remarkable peak in the Bauhaus agenda of implementing works.

Institute for Advanced Architecture of Catalonia (IAAC), Endesa Pavilion, Barcelona, 2011

top right: The southwest facade showing the location-specific positioning of solar panels.

Hulvågen Bridges, Atlantic Road National Tourist Route, Møre og Romsdal, Norway

View of two of the eight bridges that connect the small islands along the route, the most prominent of which is the Storseisundet Bridge – which can be seen in the background.

Rural Studio, 20K Houses, Greensboro, Hale County, Alabama, 2008

The Pattern Book House, Loft House and Roundwood House demonstrate the diversity of designs within Rural Studio's 20K Houses research programme.

Shin Egashira/
Koshirakura
Landscape
Workshop,
Bus shelter,
Koshirakura,
Tōkamachi,
Niigata,
Japan,
1997

The bus shelter
in summer.

Scarcity and
Creativity
Studio
(SCL), Las
Piedras
del Cielo,
Open City,
Ritoque,
Chile,
2012

Experimental
landform structures
and canopies are
recurrent themes
in projects by
the Scarcity and
Creativity Studio
at the Oslo School
of Architecture and
Design (AHO).

Studio Mumbai
workshop,
Mumbai,
2012

The workshop
courtyard where
material samples,
models and mock-
ups are displayed.

Open City,
Ritoque,
Chile,
2012

View of the lower-
lying areas of
the Open City in
the coastal dune
landscape of the
Pacific.

18th century gradually led to the understanding that 'architecture should be firmly based on specific regional practices based on climate, geography, local materials, and local traditions. It has been tacitly assumed that such a foundation is necessary for the development of an authentic modern architecture.'[3] Yet he cautions that

> the concept of regionality depends on it being possible to correlate cultural codes with geographical regions. It is based on traditional systems of communication in which climate, geography, craft traditions, and religions are absolutely determining. These determinants are rapidly disappearing and in large parts of the world no longer exist ... Modern society is polyvalent – that is to say, its codes are generated randomly from within a universal system of rationalisation.[4]

The outcome of the multitude of individual codes that supplanted the consistency of the regional deployment of the local can be seen in the plethora of idiosyncratic architectures today. In terms of Frampton's definition of critical regionalism, a possible solution was to be found in avoiding conservatism and subjecting modern architecture to a series of strategies that would foster a merger between contemporaneous and local drivers for architectural design: 'to mediate the impact of universal civilisation with elements derived indirectly from the peculiarities of a particular place'.[5] Moving on from critical regionalism, a number of thought-provoking questions arise. For architecture to be intensely local while avoiding rampant individualism, is an overarching regional approach necessary to ensure the relevance of designs vis-à-vis local circumstances? To what extent do architectures of a particular locality need to share traits? Do the shared traits necessarily involve a particular 'look', or can they be located in aspects such as the provisions architecture makes for locally specific patterns of use and habitation, its performative capacities in relation to the local setting, and modes of designing and building that relate to or animate local activities?

And what might be thought of as 'local' sensibilities?[6] The approaches to locally specific architectures outlined in this issue of ⌂ seem motivated not to revive critical regionalism, but rather to explore shifts in design attitudes from which 'schools of thought' emerge that operate on unique combinations of setting, client, resources, materials and designers. Where present architecture mainly operates on standardisation and individualistic expression, the architectures highlighted here experiment with designs born out of local circumstances that share the search for qualitative traits that rest outside current frameworks of standardisation. This also opens up ways of redeploying the 'non-standard architecture' approach (see pp 110–15), in that its latent potential lies not in superficial individualism but, instead, in its capacity to be informed by design criteria pertaining to local conditions. Here, then, it becomes possible to negotiate contemporary technological development with the need to develop contemporary local architectures.

In 'Past and Present Trajectories of Experimental Architectures' (pp 16–23), we review some of the predominant ways in which experimental architectures arise, either as part of events such as fairs, expos and sequenced projects, or, alternatively, through the sustained efforts of dedicated groups, schools or practices. We also distinguish here between experimental projects with and without local specificity. In 'Building In and Out of Place' (pp 24–9), David Leatherbarrow discusses the fact that any construction is a transformation that in one way or another renders the local specific by way of change. Barbara Elisabeth Ascher (pp 30–33) examines the intentions of the early Bauhaus syllabus in teaching students skills in various crafts and emphasising involvement in the making of architectures.

The subsequent articles feature selected projects that accumulate over time either in one location or in a geographically more dispersed yet

strategic manner. With David Jolly Monge we look at the Open City in Ritoque, Chile, where the School of Architecture and Design at the Pontifical Catholic University of Valparaíso pursues its search for a local architecture (pp 34–9). The two-decade-long development and work of Rural Studio at Auburn University in Alabama is then examined (pp 40–47), followed by a discussion of the work of the Scarcity and Creativity Studio (SCL) at the Oslo School of Architecture and Design (AHO) (pp 48–57), which operates on differences in latitude and locality. Shin Egashira then outlines the work of the Koshirakura Landscape Workshop in Japan (pp 58–63). Karl Otto Ellefsen discusses the strategic intentions that underlie the Norwegian National Tourist Routes project, illustrated by a number of the architectural installations and interventions along the way (pp 64–75). The two following articles review similar developments and the focus by two Norwegian firms on small projects as a locus for experimental and locally specific works. The first is on the work of Rintala Eggertson Architects (pp 76–81), and Lisbet Harboe then introduces the young practice TYIN tegnestue (pp 82–7).

The discussion then moves on to contemporary modes of operation and working methods. The articles here delve further into the field of architectural practice and experimental approaches. The formative years and related key works of the Renzo Piano Building Workshop are discussed by Peter Buchanan (pp 88–93). This is followed by a look at the work of Studio Mumbai with its explicit conversational mode of design and close integration of craftsmen within the design process (pp 94–101). Philip Nobel describes how computational approaches and making are integrated within the work of SHoP Architects (pp 102–9), and Søren S Sørensen examines the way in which a rethought and informed non-standard approach to architecture can facilitate locally specific designs (pp 110–15). The notion of auxiliary architectures and how supplementation of the existing built environment can improve the location-specific performative capacity of already existing architectures is then discussed on pp 116–19. Defne Sunguroğlu Hensel and Guillem Baraut Bover illustrate Nested Catenaries, an innovative construction system made from brick that references historic cases and is developed through prototypes into a structural system that can be adapted to locally specific circumstances (pp 120–27). Likewise, Rodrigo Rubio and Areti Markopoulou's article on the Institute for Advanced Architecture of Catalonia's Endesa Pavilion in Barcelona (pp 128–31) introduces a solar prototype that can be adapted to local circumstances. Finally, we provide a brief outlook on the questions and further thoughts that arise out of the intersection between the different contributions.

Emerging Contours

The aim of the issue is to examine different facets of the discipline of architecture including educational frameworks, practices and various hybrid setups, and also to try to address the possibilities in contemporary design methods and materialisation processes for intensely local architectures. However, a comprehensive overview is neither feasible nor intended; the objective is not to declare a new 'style' or 'ism', but instead to portray the continuous development required to maintain the capacity to address the ever-changing conditions of local settings, and the variety of promising approaches and themes from the intersection of which may arise interesting questions and insights. Undertaking this work has been on many levels extraordinarily inspiring and informative, as the contours of a contemporary multifaceted approach to intensely local architectures gradually begin to emerge. Clearly this is but a snapshot in time, and continual efforts need to ensue to keep rethinking intensely local architectures through experimental constructions. It is our hope to inspire the reader to engage in this task. ᴆ

Notes
1. See for instance Mari Hvattum, *Gottfried Semper and the Problem of Historicism*, Cambridge University Press (Cambridge), 2004.
2. Kenneth Frampton, *Studies in Tectonic Culture: The Poetics of Construction in Nineteenth and Twentieth Century Architecture*, MIT Press (Cambridge, MA), 1995, pp 5–6.
3. Alan Colquhoun, 'Critique of Regionalism', in Vincent B Canizaro (ed), *Architectural Regionalism: Collected Writings on Place, Identity, Modernity, and Tradition*, Princeton Architectural Press (New York), 2007 [1996], p 141.
4. *Ibid*, p 154.
5. Kenneth Frampton, 'Towards a Critical Regionalism: Six Points for an Architecture of Resistance', in Hal Foster (ed), *The Anti-Aesthetic: Essays on Postmodern Culture*, Bay Press (Port Townsend, WA), 1983, p 21.
6. The question regarding local sensibilities and architectures also motivated two previous issue of ᴆ: Michael Hensel and Defne Sunguroğlu Hensel (eds), *ᴆ Turkey: At the Threshold*, January/February (no 1), 2010 and Michael Hensel and Mehran Gharleghi, *ᴆ Iran: Past, Present and Future*, May/June (no 3), 2012.

Defne Sunguroğlu Hensel and Guillem Baraut Bover, Nested Catenaries, Open City, Ritoque, Chile, 2012

View of the site-specific iteration of the design system adjacent to the cemetery at the Open City.

OCEAN Design Research Association and Izmir University of Economy, Luminous Veil, Izmir, Turkey, 2009

The textile screen wall at different times of the day showing the installation's capacity for light modulation and amplification.

Michael Hensel and
Christian Hermansen Cordua

Joseph Paxton,
The Crystal Palace,
Hyde Park, London,
1851

The Crystal Palace
from the northeast,
from *Dickinsons'
Comprehensive Pictures
of the Great Exhibition
of 1851*, published
in 1854.

Past and Present Trajectories of Experimental Architectures

As architects compete on the world stage through the very diversity and disparateness of their expression, how might it be possible to develop an experimental approach that has value and credibility at a local level? Guest-Editors **Michael Hensel and Christian Hermansen Cordua** explore the possibilities for locally specific experimental architecture – past and present.

Difference, which used to be ensured by the co-existence of ... autonomous regions of culture, now depends largely on two other phenomena: individualism and the nation-state.

— Alan Colquhoun, 'The Concept of Regionalism', 1997[1]

How can the question of difference in local architectures be addressed in a climate of global homogenisation of the built environment and a concurrent wave of proliferating individualism in architectural design? What could be a promising approach? And could experimental architectures play a role in this, instead of resorting to either fatalism or conservatism? Experimental works span a wide range from paper architectures that illustrate utopian or dystopian visions, which may not necessarily be intended for realisation or to even be realisable, to works that are clearly intended for implementation and demonstrate the application of novel ideas and approaches in full scale with all the associated risks and consequences. But which of these works may feasibly provide an inroad to contemporary locally specific architectures? To gain an understanding it is necessary to differentiate between the trajectories of experimental architectures that pursue varying objectives.

The first and more universal trajectory has come into full command over a century and a half, in the wake of the broad industrialisation of all production sectors, by way of an increasing range of high-profile international events such as world's fairs and expos that have yielded many exceptional experimental projects. These include vast iconic structures such as Joseph Paxton's Crystal Palace in London (1851) or Gustave Eiffel's Tower in Paris (1889), as well as individual exemplary pavilions. Both types of project frequently profited in their architectural expression from materials and elements produced through new industrial processes. The world's fairs were paralleled by similar events including the International Exposition of Modern Industrial and Decorative Arts in Paris (1925),[2] and the Deutscher Werkbund exhibitions.

Bruno Taut,
Glasshouse
Pavilion,
Deutscher Werkbund
exhibition,
Cologne,
1914

Peter Behrens,
Poster design
for the Deutscher
Werkbund
exhibition,
Cologne,
1914

Le Corbusier,
Semi-detached
house,
Deutscher
Werkbund
exhibition,
Weissenhof
Siedlung,
Stuttgart,
1927

Founded in 1907
by Hermann
Muthesius, the
Deutscher Werkbund
resulted in a
series of landmark
exhibitions, most
notably in 1914 in
Cologne, and the
1927 exhibition in
Stuttgart.

The Deutscher Werkbund was an association of architects, artists, designers and industrialists, founded in 1907 that sought to engage designers and manufacturers in a close productive partnership.

The Deutscher Werkbund was an association of architects, artists, designers and industrialists, founded in 1907 that sought to engage designers and manufacturers in a close productive partnership. Notable exhibitions that showcased seminal works took place in Cologne in 1914 and Stuttgart in 1927. Related to this was the development of the Bauhaus with its initial endeavour to educate students by way of engagement in construction. There was also an explicit trajectory of individual research-oriented experimental architectures that included notable projects such as Richard Buckminster Fuller's Dymaxion House (1930), the works of Jean Prouvé such as Maison Tropicale (1949), his prefabricated petrol stations (1953) and Plastic House (1965), and Matti Suuronen's Futuro Houses (late 1960s). Occasionally, individual efforts were part of larger frameworks, for example the Case Study Houses programme sponsored by *Arts & Architecture* magazine, which ran from 1945 to 1966.

In a similar way to the world's fairs, frequent garden and horticultural expos also attracted architectural experimentation. Originating from 18th-century English and French garden and landscape design, the folly, a building type mainly for decorative purposes, was repurposed in a contemporary manner by cities and regions that sought to profile themselves through idiosyncratic architectures by 'star' architects. In the early 1990s, numerous follies appeared, most notably in the Netherlands and at the International Garden and Greenery Expo in Osaka.[3] A decade later, in 2000, a new series of prominent architectural experiments was launched in the format of the annual pavilions at, for instance, the Serpentine Gallery in London. Such events promoted wider trends and developments such as idiosyncratic architectural design, which gradually became a form of branding in which to some extent the element of the experimental shifted out of focus and made way for what might be more appropriately termed styling. Another dominant aspect of architectures generated for the events and fairs discussed above is an obvious habitual foregrounding of what is possible, rather than addressing the local.

Bernard Tschumi,
Glass Video
Gallery,
Groningen,
The Netherlands,
1990

Although originally
constructed as a
temporary structure
for a music and video
festival in Groningen
in 1990, the small
iconic building was
kept on site.

Within this context, what can be gleaned is a gradual shift in experimental works from promoting technological advances to addressing pressing contemporary questions of architectural provisions on a mass scale, and eventually to individual expression for the main purpose of branding and styling. The experimental aspect is clearly present here, but to what end when recognisable 'style' is required and thus turns into constraint?

Though there are noteworthy exceptions of architectures at such events that engage local specificity or at least point towards ways of doing so, experimental works that consider the local generally tend to occur outside of high-profile international fairs. Instead they are often part of long-term accumulative projects that make no claim to universal applicability, for example the Open City in Ritoque, Chile (see pp 34–9), the works of Rural Studio in Alabama (pp 40–47), the initial works at Hooke Park in Dorset conceived as a forest campus previously owned by the Parnham Trust's School for Woodland Industries, and perhaps also the Norwegian National Tourist Routes scheme with its distributed projects (pp 64–75). Locally specific design criteria may vary between projects within and also between such larger schemes. The Open City projects continually seek an updated architecture of Pacific South America that takes into consideration the local landscape and culture. Rural Studio addresses questions of local social problems and the specific situation of the particular people it makes provisions for. The initial projects for the woodland campus of Hooke Park evolved around questions of combined woodland preservation and industrial forestry, as well as the use of low-construction-grade timber in architecture. The

Coop Himmelb(l)au,
Video Clip Folly,
Groningen,
The Netherlands,
1990

Numerous experimental follies and pavilions were commissioned in the Netherlands during the 1990s.

Norwegian National Tourist Routes projects aim to accentuate the specific local landscape conditions and in so doing promote promising Norwegian practices through works that display a distinctly Norwegian flavour. In general, this trajectory of experimental architecture is currently not discussed in broader terms, although it points towards an interesting possibility and is becoming increasingly widespread.

How may we then define the 'local'? Needless to say, the intent is not to revive outdated notions of contextualism or regionalism. However, in order to set out an argument it is useful to briefly look back. Interestingly, Kenneth Frampton pointed out that:

> Two interrelated factors are of ultimate importance when we consider the idea of region from an institutional standpoint. The first of these may be subsumed under the notion of discourse; the second addresses itself to the cultivation of the client in a profound sense. By *discourse* I mean first and foremost the coming into being of a 'school' of local culture, although my use of the term 'school' has wider connotations as well. Nonetheless, this idea returns us to the critical importance of the architectural school as a pedagogical *and* cultural institution. By 'client', I intend only to remind you of the obvious – namely, that a culturally significant work can hardly be achieved without a committed client.[4]

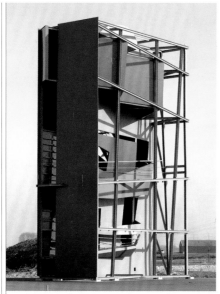

Zaha Hadid,
Video Pavilion,
Appingedam,
The Netherlands,
1990, rebuilt
2008

The original pavilion
from 1990 was
demolished and
reconstructed in 2008.

Boris Ivelic,
Entrance lodge
and Wind Harp
installation,
Hospedería de la
Entrada y Arpa
Eólica, Open
City, Ritoque,
Chile,
1985

The works at the Open
City are diverse in their
individual expression
while at the same time
cohering to a shared
spatial sensibility and
material articulation.
This innate coherent
yet open-ended
pluralism constitutes a
recognisable school of
thought in the search for
a Chilean Pacific coastal
architecture.

*Local specificity
does not entail
uniformity in
design. Different
schools of thought
can coexist and
compete to prevent
homogenisation
and stagnation.*

Ahrends, Burton,
Koralek (ABK),
Frei Otto and
Buro Happold,
Workshop,
Hooke Park,
Dorset, England,
1989

The workshop design is
based on wooden arches
that are pre-stressed
through bending.

Notes
1. Alan Colquhoun, 'The Concept of Regionalism', in Vincent B Canizaro (ed), *Architectural Regionalism: Collected Writings on Place, Identity, Modernity, and Tradition,* Princeton Architectural Press (New York), 2007 [1997], p 152.
2. Notable projects at the International Exposition of Modern Industrial and Decorative Arts in 1925 included Le Corbusier's Esprit Nouveau, as well as Konstantin Melnikov's Soviet Pavilion and Alexander Rodchenko's Workers' Club. The contributions of the latter two represented the most prominent participation at this type of event of faculty from Vkhutemas, the Russian State Art and Technical School in Moscow founded in 1920 and the centre of development of Russian avant-garde Rationalism, Constructivism and Suprematism.
3. For a well-illustrated account see *Osaka Follies,* Architectural Association (London), 1991.
4. Kenneth Frampton, 'Ten Points on an Architecture of Regionalism: A Provisional Polemic', in Vincent B Canizaro, op cit, p 380.

Ahrends, Burton, Koralek (ABK), Frei Otto and Buro Happold, Refectory, Hooke Park, Dorset, England, 1987

The refectory was the first building of the Hooke Park campus. Round-wood thinnings are used in the roof, utilising their tensile strength.

A number of the frameworks within which the work discussed in this issue of *D* is produced are directly related to, or literally part of, schools of architecture: the Open City, Rural Studio, Scarcity and Creativity Studio (see pp 48–57) and Koshirakura Landscape Workshop (pp 58–63). In these contexts, the joint aspects of 'pedagogical *and* cultural' are foregrounded in different ways. However, these are not schools in the regional sense, as discussed by Frampton. Instead they are 'schools of thought' in architectural design that address the question of the local in different ways, for different purposes and with different consequences. They can benefit from operating in an experimental modus in two ways: first by avoiding traditionalist tendencies in favour of continually rethinking local specificity, and second by opening up the project brief in a manner that changes their stakeholdership to co-client status.

Thus, local specificity does not entail uniformity in design. Different schools of thought can coexist and compete to prevent homogenisation and stagnation. The driver of differences in local architectures may therefore be shifted from that of individual expression and style to one of a pluralism of schools of thought and design languages.

This may also present a way of reinvigorating some of the increasingly moribund events by carefully analysing and engaging individual efforts in architectural experimentation within sets of shared objectives, while at the same time looking out for unusual traits in different approaches to the question of the local. This may well involve the question again of technical advances as some of the examples in this issue of *D* highlight, such as the Informed Non-Standard approach discussed by Søren S Sørensen (see pp 110–15), the Nested Catenaries project by Defne Sunguroğlu Hensel and Guillem Baraut Bover (pp 120–27) and the Endesa Pavilion by the Institute for Advanced Architecture of Catalonia (IAAC) (pp 128–31).

All of these approaches seem to follow what one might consider particular schools of thought in addressing locality in architectural design. It is this productive pluralism that mediates between shared agendas and individual expression. If this is the case we may well be at the doorstep of a reinvigorated and well-equipped regeneration of local specificity in architectural design. *D*

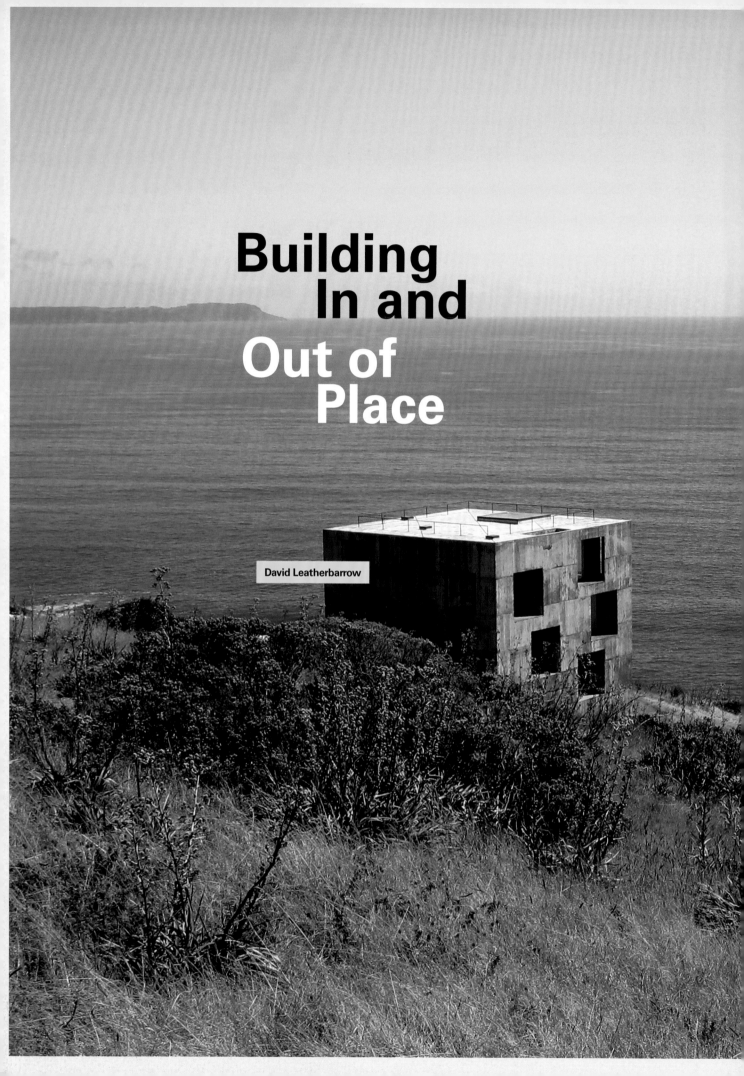

Building In and Out of Place

Out of Place

David Leatherbarrow

Pezo von Ellrichshausen,
Casa Poli, Coliumo, Chile,
2005

View from the approach road towards
the ocean showing a built within a
natural horizon.

To seize the opportunities that designing globally afford – albeit in a disorientated and displaced manner – or to continue practising at the small scale in an informed and sensitive way, is the predicament that most ambitious offices are confronted with today. Here **David Leatherbarrow**, Professor of Architecture at the University of Pennsylvania, argues that there could be a third way that manifests itself in the land itself and a project's site. He suggests terrain 'has the power to allow and to resist the dislocations we experience today, recalling what a location has been while indicating what it is becoming'.

*Nicht ohne Schwingen mag
Zum Nächsten einer greifen
Geradezu*

*[Not without wings may one
Reach out for that which is nearest
Directly]*

— Friedrich Hölderlin, *Der Ister, c* 1803–5[1]

LA DALLMAN,
Marsupial Bridge,
Milwaukee,
Wisconsin, 2002

Midway along the new
bridge, which is hung from
the pre-existing structure,
at once architectural,
infrastructural and
topographical.

Not anywhere – not only here: that is the principle that governs the siting of the better buildings of our time. While it seems perfectly natural for architects to practise locally, few today reject opportunities to build internationally, despite the fact that the knowledge that guides the first – knowledge of the local environment, history, culture and technology – is inadequate to the second, defined as it often is by a very different climate, culture and building tradition. Practices that work globally try to compensate for partial understanding by qualifying their routine methods with token representations. The results are often poor. Should foreign opportunities be rejected for that reason? Should they, instead, be embraced as the real horizon of contemporary architecture, on the assumption that so-called regional practices are mostly backward looking?

Alternatively, would a choice be sensible: each practice decide to specialise in work that is suited to the global horizon or the local context, working on types of projects that could be located anywhere or those that could be built only here? Probably not, for then knowledge developed in different places, but within the discipline, would be shared less often or lost. Because a third way seems to escape our grasp we have come to accept the compromised solutions that conflate generalised techniques with particularised interpretations.

In a time of fast-paced globalisation and self-assured localism, one is thus led to ask about the real power and significance of terrain, the actual terrain in which buildings, landscapes and parts of cities are built. What does the work's location actually signify and what force does it really exercise over an architect's design? My answer, briefly stated, is this: the power of terrain today is its capacity to simultaneously resist and allow the ambitions of design, particularly its representational ambitions. The site's capacity to signify is not a part of the issue that I want to oppose or neglect, only postpone. The condition I want to begin with instead is the constructed aspect of buildings and landscapes, the fact that they are made. My opening point is simple: sites with cultural significance must be built.[2] While there may be nothing controversial in this statement, it is a truism that still merits thought. Such is the aim of my opening suggestion: the labour involved in site construction is what terrain both resists and allows.

Grafton Architects,
Department of
Finance, Dublin,
2007

The corner of St Stephen's
Green showing how the
building contributes to the
redefinition of its place – both
the Green and the tiny garden
at its side.

My next point will also seem plain: every built project is built somewhere, in some location that is not only territorial, but also dynamic. With this last term I mean subject to an interplay of forces – environmental and social – that encompass and reshape what gets built, even though they are often unapparent and exercise their effects over long periods of time. The key, of course, is to grasp the nature of this interplay, particularly its schedules (before, during and after construction) and its distances (in the project's vicinity, neighbourhood and wider horizons). One of the most challenging developments of the last few years in the arts I call 'topographical' – architecture, landscape architecture and urban design – is the reconsideration of the relationships between representation and performance. For many designers today the first (representation) is thought to be largely determined by the second (performance or operation).[3] Accordingly, built works look the way they do because of the ways they behave, at least largely so, for figurative, even representational aims are never avoided entirely. Here then is my third premise: the interplay of powers that define both the place and the project determine the work's significance.

Now my last introductory point: local terrain is what the project is not. To make sense of this simple statement one must try to overcome two longstanding commonplaces: that the locations that hold significance are the ones that are familiar to us, and that the projects that make them so are somehow native to the place in which they are constructed. I say 'try to' overcome these notions because they are too longstanding to be overcome easily. But if architecture, landscape architecture and urban design are to be seen as arts – the results of constructive intentions and practices – the related ideas of meaning-as-recognition and construction-as-cultivation need to be surpassed. When I describe terrain as what the project is not, I point to the latter's essential artificiality. Dislocation is the result. Through design, places become what they were not, come to exist outside themselves.

Let me elaborate this point a little. Designs that intend congeniality with pre-existing terrain tend to focus on the aspects of a place that are directly perceptible. No one can sensibly maintain that terrain is without form or physicality, nor that it is imperceptible; it is a matter of fact – perhaps the very matter of fact. Yet dedication to what presents itself immediately often neglects the less obvious forces at play in the constitution, development and deterioration of what we see, forces I have characterised as environmental and social. Neglect for constitutive forces corresponds to concentration on the signifying, not the dynamic aspects, of terrain.

Project making's basic task, however, is to discover something new in the site, something not already there.[4] When that is not done there is no project, still less currency of sense. And what is discovered comes into visibility through labour, the labour of design and construction. But just as designs that intend congeniality with place overlook opportunities for creative transformation, those that import something new to the place, something developed in isolation from existing conditions and constraints, also miss the point. Design work of this second, non-place-bound sort is sometimes called experimental. Its results arise out of the instruments of design themselves. Precisely because of its instrumental nature it remains indifferent to the project's actual conditions, for technical procedures are essentially non-territorial. But there is another kind of experimental practice, an engaged or involved way of working in which the play with possibilities is constrained by existing conditions. In practices of this sort the new emerges from the familiar. Why or how? Because the world in which design finds its place has greater potential than past projects had imagined.

Yi-Chun Chen, Dragon Art Museum, Shanghai, 2013

left: Diagonal view across the entry court, including a fragment of a pre-existing structure with which the new building coincides and contrasts.

O'Donnell + Tuomey, LSE Student Centre, London, 2014

right: View from Lincoln's Inn Fields, discovering unforeseen but intelligible height, geometry and scale within the urban location.

Land, Scape and Landscape

A hint about the constructed nature of culturally significant terrain can be gleaned from old linguistic usage; specifically the tensions between three understandings of the word 'landscape': its scenic or aesthetic sense, its territorial meaning, and the idea of landscape as a domain for social, community or civic life. Explaining these meanings briefly will help me develop my point about the constructed nature of locations with cultural significance.

The suffix 'scape' is cognate with 'scope' and sustains all the interpretations that accent the visual aspects of terrain; hence the longstanding sense of the landscape as pictorial subject matter. Yet the German equivalent, *'schaft'*, like its English cognate 'ship', points not to something that is primarily visual, but something made. In their verb forms these terms mean to build or create, as in *'schaffen'*. The old sense of the nouns, on the other hand, can be seen in the ties between the words 'ship' and 'shape'. A township, for example, was a body politic formed under law as well as the territorial domain shaped by those citizens. As for the first half of the term, the history of meanings conveyed by the word 'land' (in its several European variants) also couples territory with structures of coexistence. A given stretch of territory would be called 'land' because of its legal system or style of governance as much as by its physical characteristics – and when those were considered, climate was as important as ground area.

Land was defined by laws and customs, giving rise to cultural identity; thus, the English, Danish or German lands were characterised principally by ways of living. In the 18th century, Johann Gottfried von Herder's coupling of the ways of a people *(Volk)* and the characteristics of their place and climate expressed the territorial and political sense of land very well.[5] The many 19th-century variants of this thesis – including the materialistic coupling of place and race, which provided a pseudo-rationale for the wars and terror of the 20th century – both extended and distorted this same premise. An earlier and benign articulation of land in this double sense can be seen, oddly enough, when paintings are considered. Sixteenth-century landscape painting, particularly in Holland, but also in Germany, often portrayed local customs – marrying, trading and dining – to identify the characteristics of communities that were beginning to take a stand against the Roman Catholic Church and its universalising ambitions. The contemporaries of Pieter Brueghel the Elder (*c* 1525–69) saw his paintings as 'pregnant with whole provinces'.[6] We see not only the layout and look of terrain, but the prosaic activities that typically occur there.

This point can be made negatively: the great German artist Albrecht Altdorfer (1480–1538) has been described as the first modern landscape painter because many of his scenes omit all indications of local custom and life, as they do religious themes, concentrating instead on water, soil, vegetation and sky. Traditional subject matter was distinguished from its setting and then replaced by it. What had been the background or supplement became the foreground, though in a fictive, rather than documentary, sense. Before this time, however, the polar opposite to land was not sea, as with terrain in the Latin languages, but forest, because it had not been appropriated into the patterns of society, had not been made fit for life, its dynamism and cultural norms.

All of the meanings of 'land', 'scape' and 'landscape' I have parsed out are available for contemporary use. The range allows today's writers and designers to alternately emphasise the visual, physical, environmental or social aspects of architecture and landscape. Because so much stress was placed on the visual and signifying sense of built terrain in recent decades, contemporary work has re-emphasised topography's performative sense, its environmental and social operations.

Not Anywhere – Not Only Here

I recommend we extend and develop this recent style of thinking, but concentrate not so much on the material aspects of projects – discussed so commonly these days – but on their configurational dimensions; specifically, the mosaic heterogeneity, the internal discordance of works that tolerate discontinuous or displaced settings within their expanse, areas that could be called 'uncommon grounds'.[7] I have in mind locations in which one is removed from a given area's familiar horizon and relocated to some distant place, a foreign terrain or country, for example, or some distant time, without, of course, actually going elsewhere. Displacement such as this occurs thanks to the qualities of the work as a work, its constructive or fictive character, made and made up. Concrete though it is, such an experience is indefinite. Terrain, I want to suggest, has the power to allow and to resist the dislocations we experience today, recalling what a location has been while indicating what it is becoming.

Albrecht Altdorfer,
*Landscape with Large
Fir (Larch) Tree,*
c 1522

right: In Altdorfer's works, traditional subject matter was distinguished from its setting and then replaced by it.

Pieter Brueghel
the Elder, *The
Netherlandish Proverbs,*
1559

left: In Brueghel's works, we see not only the layout and look of terrain, but the prosaic activities that typically occur there.

Reorientation

When projects take up a conversation with pre-existing conditions they generally succeed in making some of their points apparent; but in the course of the dialogue they also suffer some unexpected assertions, different forms of mis-maintenance, over- or under-growth and reuse that tends towards misuse. These changes make sense retrospectively, but were not foreseen at the outset. The labours of design and construction should not for that reason be judged unsuccessful, especially when the innovations or discordances themselves were forceful, for the 'original' intentions and accomplishments survive in part, despite re-qualifications that augment the sense of the place and free it into kinds of significance that could not have been realised anywhere, but were not defined by meanings assumed to exist only there. Freedom of that sort – design's greatest task – finds its foothold in conditions that are both specific to the project and seen otherwise, thanks to the qualities of the work itself. I call this 'architecture oriented otherwise'.

Five simple points can summarise the characteristics and promise of architecture that is built in and out of its place: (1) Locations obtain cultural significance through construction, not by nature; sites are not developed, but discovered through design and construction; (2) Although environmental and social powers are always at play in the locations of construction, their interplay must be structured by design, not, though, the sort of design that amplifies one or the other independently; (3) Because project making's basic task is to bring something new to its location, the discordances that result make the location into something it was not; a successful work is always part of and apart from its location; (4) The creative coupling of pre-existing with desired, but unprecedented, conditions holds the key to renewing topographical meaning; and (5) Once absorbed into the cultural practices of a location, previously discordant insertions come to be seen as natural, eventually inviting and then suffering future transformations. ∆

Notes
1. Friedrich Hölderlin, 'The Ister', *Friedrich Hölderlin: Poems & Fragments*, trans Michael Hamburger, Anvil Press Poetry (London), 1966, p 513.
2. Obvious examples would include the High Line in New York City (James Corner Field Operations and Diller Scofidio + Renfro, 2014), the Seattle Art Museum Olympic Sculpture Park (Weiss/Manfredi, 2007), the Oslo Opera House (Snøhetta, 2008) or the Brazilian Museum of Sculpture in São Paulo (Paulo Mendes da Rocha, 1988).
3. Several recent publications attest to the widespread interest in 'performance' as a theme, as well as the idea that it holds the key to representation. See, for example: Branko Kolaravic and Ali Malkawi, *Performative Architecture: Beyond Instrumentality*, Routledge (London), 2005, which demonstrates the argument about performance through discussion of projects of figures such as Jean Nouvel, Norman Foster, Thomas Herzog and Renzo Piano.
4. Consider, for example, the following cases in which design and construction did not 'fit into' the location, but discovered its specific and unforeseen possibilities: LA DALLMAN's Marsupial Bridge (Milwaukee, 2002), illustrated herein; Eric Parry's St Martin-in-the-Field remodelling (London, 2008); or historically, Lina Bo Bardi's SESC Pompéia in São Paulo (1982) or Sverre Fehn's Hedmark Museum in Hamar, Norway (1967–79).
5. The topic is fully addressed in Frederick M Bernard, *Herder on Nationality, Humanity, and History*, McGill-Queen's University Press (Montreal), 2003.
6. See Kenneth R Olwig, 'Recovering the Substantive Nature of Landscape', *Annals of the Association of American Geographers*, 86, 4, December 1996, p 634.
7. I use this term in the sense I developed in *Uncommon Ground: Architecture, Technology, and Topography*, MIT Press (Cambridge, MA), 2000. Architects who practised in different parts of the world are discussed in that book; well-known figures such as Le Corbusier and Frank Lloyd Wright, but also others who are less commonly studied: Richard Neutra (in the US), Aris Konstantinidis (in Greece) and Antonin Raymond (in Japan). What holds them in common and makes comparisons useful is that each of them confronted the problem of coordinating widely distributed elements and technologies with local conditions.

Pezo von Ellrichshausen, Casa Poli, Coliumo, Chile, 2005

View from the slope into the shore towards a construction that is no less rugged than the stone on which it stands, despite its highly refined geometry.

Steven Holl, Nelson–Atkins Museum of Art, Kansas City, Missouri, 2007

View across the several topographical levels the building has restructured.

Wang Shu and Lu Wenyu (Amateur Architecture Studio), Wa Shan Guesthouse, China Academy of Art, Hangzhou, China, 2014

View at the entry, coupling pre-existing landform with unprecedented built form.

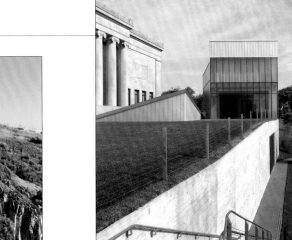

Barbara Elisabeth Ascher

With its strong emphasis on students acquiring practical, craft skills alongside more formal design expertise, the Bauhaus provides a significant 20th-century precedent for current schools of architecture focusing on learning through making. Architect and urban planner **Barbara Elisabeth Ascher** describes how the approach to pedagogy in architecture evolved during the Bauhaus's 14-year history (1919–33), and the shift in leadership from Walter Gropius to Hannes Meyer and then finally to Ludwig Mies van der Rohe.

the bauhaus

case study experiments in education

Advertisement for the Bauhaus in Dessau published in *Die Weltbühne*, 1925

The advertisement outlines the various stages of the educational programme including a trial work for practice.

Walter Gropius

Graph of the educational process at the Bauhaus

1923

The formal and practical formation at the Bauhaus centred around 'building' as the cornerstone of a close collaboration between arts and architecture. Redrawn by the author. Original graph first published in Walter Gropius, *Idee und Aufbau des Staatlichen Bauhauses Weimar*, Bauhausverlag (Munich), 1923, p 4.

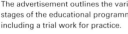

Walter Gropius, Adolf
Meyer and Georg Muche

Haus am Horn,
Bauhaus exhibition

Weimar, Germany

1923

top: Designed and built for the
Bauhaus exhibition in 1923, the
Haus am Horn brought together
designs made in the various
workshops at the Bauhaus.

bottom: Both the kitchen interior,
designed by Benita Otte and
Ernst Gebhardt, as well as the
accompanying various ceramic
objects were considered an
integral part of the model home.

the complete building is the final aim of the visual arts. their noblest function was once the decoration of buildings. they were inseparable parts of the great art of building. today they exist in isolation, from which they can be rescued only through the conscious, co-operative effort of all craftsmen.
— **Walter Gropius, 'Bauhaus Manifesto', 1919**[1]

An ambitious project for the reformation of education within arts and architecture was heralded through the 'Bauhaus Manifesto', which called for a new unity between the different visual arts such as painting, sculpture and architecture. It declared that the Bauhaus – in German with an obvious reference to *Bauhütte* (the medieval masonry guilds) – should become an institution that would teach and practise close cooperation between the different arts and would enable them to merge into innovative designs and, as the ultimate goal, into architecture.

Walter Gropius, one of the driving forces behind the establishment of the Bauhaus in Weimar, strongly believed in a reformed pedagogy for architectural education that would bridge the gap between the artist and the craftsman and would bring it back to its origins in the medieval guilds – multidisciplinary working cooperatives whose impressive skills were strongly based on international knowledge transfer and a large degree of practical experience.

The establishment of a building laboratory was a cornerstone of the Bauhaus programme complementing an arts and crafts education that would begin with a general introduction to materials, form and colour, and training in different workshops and artists' studios. As Gropius wrote in a job offer to Emil Lange, an architect and leader of the Bauhütte Breslau: 'We intend to establish a large-scale experimental studio where practical workshop problems may be addressed in both the technical and formal senses, under the direction of a highly qualified practicing architect. Such an experimental studio would stay in contact with the architectural commissions received by the Bauhaus or by myself.'[2] The organisational model for case-study experiments thus did not differentiate between commissions for the private architectural offices of their directors and teachers, and commissions for the Bauhaus institution, as in the well-known Haus Sommerfeld in Berlin.

Between Formal and Practical Education: the Full-Scale Case Studies

Oskar Schlemmer, master at the sculpture workshop, complained to his friend Otto Meyer in a letter in March 1922 that 'these commissions, factories, individual houses, more or less well solved, consequently constitute the thing about which everything else is supposed to revolve. It is an architecture business, contrasting with the scholastic function of a workshop.'[3] Though the planned *Bauversuchsplatz* (building laboratory) was never realised due to the overstretched financial situation in which the Bauhaus at Weimar found itself, the idea of a Bauhaus building estate was very much alive, and was developed further in an architectural class along with the idea of housing based on combinations of modules or a 'large-scale building set'. It finally came together in a full-scale case study of a model home for the Bauhaus exhibition in 1923. Exhibited under the title 'Arts and technology – a new unity', the Haus am Horn was designed as a showcase for the skills and products of the school with the strong involvement of all the workshops. Due to financial and legal reasons, the design for this compact single-family home by Bauhaus teacher Georg Muche was carried out as a collaboration with Adolf Meyer's architectural office, and supervised by project leader Walter Morch.[4] The workshops contributed with textiles, furniture, pottery, lamps, architectural fixtures, wall painting and a fully equipped kitchen. Although commercial companies erected the building, the architects managed to integrate some experimentation through the use of innovative materials such as Torfoleum insulation and Jurko plates.

While the result certainly had elements of a *Gesamtkunstwerk* (total work of art), subtle differences between the role of the workshops and that of studio teaching in regard to architectural education began to emerge. Architecture students were not working on the building site as their 'workshop', but assisted formally in the design of the project on paper. Interestingly, this is one of the main questions in the reply of Emil Lange to Gropius's job offer, as he sees that Gropius draws a distinction 'between the artist form masters and myself. This makes it clear that in the field of architecture – and I mean architecture in the sense of your Bauhaus programme – you also draw a distinct line between formal and practical components. I myself, just like your Bauhaus programme, do not recognise such distinction.'[5]

Walter Gropius

Bauhaus building

Dessau, Germany

1926

top and centre:
The Bauhaus building, designed and carried out by the architectural office of its director Walter Gropius, soon became an icon for the successful collaboration between architects, designers, craftspeople and artists.

Walter Gropius

Masters' Houses

Dessau, Germany

1929

bottom: This detached house for the masters Wassily Kandinsky and Paul Klee was designed by Gropius as part of a series of four experimental homes for the teaching staff of the Bauhaus.

Hannes Meyer

Federal School of the
German Trade Unions

Bernau, Berlin

1928–30

top: Based on a winning
competition entry designed
by Bauhaus students in the
Bauatelier, the school was the
work of the architectural office of
Hannes Meyer with the help of
several students as interns.

Hannes Meyer

Balcony access houses

Dessau Törten,
Germany

1929–30

bottom: This housing project
was developed from the first
sketches to the architectural
details as part of the teaching
of the architectural education
programme at the Bauhaus,
whith a strong focus on the
translation of functional
requirements into habitable
spaces.

The Bauatelier: an Architectural Office at the Bauhaus

This distinction had never disappeared, although the close collaboration between all workshops continued after the relocation of the institution to Dessau, which the main Bauhaus building and the Masters' Houses in Dessau bear witness to. Despite the fact that architectural education had adopted a more central role at the Bauhaus under the directorship of Hannes Meyer in 1928, the idea of an experimental *Bauversuchsplatz* (building laboratory) had been replaced by a *Bauatelier* (building studio) for professional building projects that were executed by construction workers for commercial clients or in collaboration with the industry. The architect´s role was hence less of a craftsman, and more of a scientist and technician who would research the user's needs and optimal utilisation of resources and mould them into a form.

Under Meyer's guidance, his students were involved in the winning entry of the architectural competition for the Federal School of the German Trade Unions in Bernau (1928–30), while the construction planning was carried out in his office in Berlin with some Bauhaus students as interns.[6] An exception to this pattern were the five balcony access houses in Dessau Törten (1929–30), since the project was a result of Meyer's studio teaching and commissioned directly to the Bauhaus. A collective of more than 10 Bauhaus students was involved in the planning phase and the supervision of the building site.[7]

Practical Experiments at the Centre of Architectural Education

When Ludwig Mies van der Rohe took over the directorship of the Bauhaus in 1930, the approach to pedagogy in architecture shifted to a more aesthetic focus. The education again emphasised a strong practical component, as described in the promotional leaflet of the architectural school: 'all theoretical subjects taught will be accompanied by practical experiments'.[8] Due to political struggles, the forced relocation to Berlin and the dissolution of the institution in 1933, none of this was implemented. The success of the Bauhaus approach, which placed a strong emphasis on making, remained only partially realised in architecture. However, the notion that the practical experience of the craftsman and the formal experience of the artist should be combined to find an appropriate solution for the future, largely unfulfilled in 1930s Germany, introduced an important aspiration for generations to come. ◮

1. *Bauhaus 50 Years: German Exhibition,* Royal Academy of Arts (London), 1968, p 13. The text is cited according to the translation used in English sources using lowercase spelling throughout, similar to the Bauhaus's typographic style. **2.** Éva Forgács, *The Bauhaus Idea and Bauhaus Politics,* Central European University Press (Budapest), 1995, p 82. **3.** Howard Dearstyne and David Spaeth, *Inside the Bauhaus,* Rizzoli (New York), 1986, p 198. **4.** Professor Bernd Rudolf (ed), *Rekonstruktion einer Utopie: Haus am Horn,* Bauhaus-Universität, Universitätsverlag (Weimar), 2000, p 17. **5.** Éva Forgács, op cit, p 82. **6.** Peter Steininger and Günter Thoms, *Die ADGB-Bundesschule Bernau bei Berlin,* EA Seemann (Leipzig), 2013, p 12. **7.** Christine Engelmann and Christian Schädlich, *Die Bauhausbauten in Dessau,* Verlag für Bauwesen (Berlin), 1991, p 91. **8.** Hans M Wingler, *Das Bauhaus: 1919–1933 – Weimar, Dessau, Berlin,* Rasch und Dumont Schauberg (Bramsche), 1962, p 189.

Located in Ritoque on central Chile's Pacific coast, Open City is a unique community established in the 1970s by faculty members from the nearby e[ad] school of architecture at the Pontifical Catholic University of Valparaíso. Here Professor **David Jolly Monge**, a founding member of the Open City, and Guest-Editors **Christian Hermansen Cordua and Michael Hensel** describe how the construction of structures on the site offer the collective community and students alike ongoing opportunities for 'thinking, research and experimentation'.

The Open City and the e[ad] School of Architecture and Design

**Christian Hermansen Cordua,
David Jolly Monge and Michael Hensel**

Ricardo Lang Studio,
Travesía Marimenuco,
Lonquimay, Chile,
2012

The 2012 Travesía resulted in an
installation designed and built
by the Ricardo Lang Studio at
e[ad].

Open City, Ritoque,
Chile, 2012

The lower-lying coastal part of the Open City.
The green area from the centre to the right
marks the sports fields. In the centre are the
river estuary and the railway bridge that
crosses it, with the Lodge of the Wind Rose
(left) and Hanging Lodge (right).

In 1952 the Jesuit rector of the Pontifical Catholic University of Valparaíso in Chile made Alberto Cruz head of its school of architecture. To reconstruct the school, which eventually became known as e[ad], Cruz gathered a group of architects, poets and artists as teachers to form a community in a cul-de-sac in Viña del Mar. Community life reinforced their conception of architecture as a way of life, a practice continued decades later in the Open City in Ritoque.

The e[ad] community criticised contemporary architectural practice and education dominated by commercialism. In its place they proposed an architecture originating from, and understood as, a poetic act. In 1964 they published an epic poem called 'Amereida' that portrays a poetic vision of America and to this day has defined the school's mission. It is written in a form where words are signifiers as well as entities in space, a poetic style practised in ancient Greece, and adopted by French Symbolist Stéphane Mallarmé in *'Un Coup de Dés Jamais N'Abolira Le Hasard'* ('A Throw of the Dice will Never Abolish Chance') (1897), who in turn influenced Modernist movements such as the Dadaists, Surrealists and the Brazilian Noigandres group.

'Amereida' declares the poetic act, called the 'Phalène', as the origin of architecture.[1] The Phalène is a group act, the outcome of which is a poem generated collectively by its participants. Also important in e[ad]'s conception of architecture is the observation of the relations between life and space recorded through sketches and words: 'We find [in these sketches] the sensual dimension of the habitable space which has been captured at that moment, as well as the dimensions of knowledge that presented themselves on that occasion.'[2] The concretisation of the poetic image into buildings forms an integral part of e[ad]'s thinking and can be seen in two main instances. The first is the travesías, school trips to destinations in the Americas, where a Phalène is performed to generate the idea for a project that is then built on the spot in a few weeks and left as a 'gift'. Through condensing the architectural process into such a short period, the travesías are a means by which to reaffirm the potential of the Phalène.

The second is in the Open City, the site for which was bought privately by e[ad] teachers in the 1970s and consists of 270 hectares (670 acres) stretching 4.8 kilometres (3 miles) along the Pacific coast and comprising dune fields, wetlands, a river, pine forests and a diversity of flora and fauna. The site is run by the Corporación Cultural Amereida that, in a unique arrangement, lends it to e[ad] for the purpose of teaching its students poetics, workshops, experimental building and sports. The purpose of the Open City is not primarily didactic; it is to become a town, collectively owned and governed, with no private property, constructed for, and by, 'hospitality and speech' and following Amereida's poetic vision of America. Proposals for new works in the Open City emanate from individuals, but are discussed and decided on by the Corporación. This is the process by which both e[ad]'s and the Corporación's thinking, research and experimentation come to fruition.

Sala de Música
(The Music Room)

Alberto Cruz and
Juan Purcell,
Sala de Música
(The Music Room),
Open City,
Ritoque, Chile,
1972

top and bottom: The central
glowing lantern provides the
main source of natural light for
the space.

The Music Room, designed by Alberto Cruz and Juan Purcell in 1972, was the first work to be built in the Open City. It is a rectangular white box diagonally clad in timber with no fenestration except where the entrances are located. Turning its back on prioritising views of its surroundings, it focuses on itself to enhance its communal function. Natural light, introduced through a central full-height lantern, articulates and mediates the relation of space and music. The 161-square-metre (1,733-square-foot) interior is dominated by the warm tones of natural wood and by the ceiling-to-floor lantern, which is also its source of ventilation and brings inside the murmur of the Pacific's breaking waves. The movable partitions in the perimeter walls have reflective and absorbent faces, the latter covered with woven reeds harvested from the local river.

On the upper, eastern side of the Open City site is a gully that carries seasonal waters into the Pacific and in which can be found three adjoining public spaces: the Cemetery, Chapel and Amphitheatre. The landscaped surfaces of all three projects are consolidated and designed to absorb as much water as possible to minimise damage during flash floods. Further downstream, the gully is lined with highly absorbent gabions and a series of horizontal steps that slow down the flow of water.

The Cemetery, located in the upper part of the gully, was designed and built by Juan Ignacio Baixas, Jorge Sánchez and Juan Purcell between 1976 and 2002. It consists of ground surfaces of common brick and compacted soil that form gathering spaces, walking paths and stairs carefully placed to highlight the gully's fertile natural landscape.

A series of landscape elements also contributes to reducing the seasonal damage of flash floods: a device for decanting sand, a frame that splits the water stream, two canals, a paving surface that carries a blanket of water, and an exit for the water that dissipates its energy. Among these interventions and the natural landscape lie the tombs of members of the Corporación Amereida and e[ad].

The open-air Amphitheatre was designed and built by Juan Ignacio Baixas, Jorge Sánchez and Juan Purcell in 2001, and extended in 2002. A place of leisure and cultural recreation, it forms an atrium that brings together longitudinal and cross circulations. The theatre is concentric to minimise the distance between spectators and stage, and consists of a gently stepped brick esplanade. Its main feature is the canal that crosses it in an east–west direction and bisects the stage.

The Cemetery, Chapel and Amphitheatre

Juan Ignacio Baixas, Jorge Sánchez and Juan Purcell, Amphitheatre, Open City, Ritoque, Chile, 1976–2002

The amphitheatre is defined by and consolidates the sloped terrain. It is traversed by a gully made from stone-filled gabions that channels the water of flash floods from the higher-lying terrain through the theatre to a low-lying valley.

Hospedería del Errante
(Wanderer's Lodge)

Manuel Casanueva,
Second version of
Hospedería del Errante
(Wanderer's Lodge),
Open City, Ritoque,
Chile,
1995

right: The primary structure of the Wanderer's Lodge was erected in 1981, but decayed due to the impact of weather over time. The current version constitutes a rethinking and remodelling of the first, and was made possible as a research project within the framework of the Chilean National Council of Scientific Research. The research focused on two themes – light and wind – and as such the outer shell of the building is conceived as fuselages and lattices that modulate luminosity and airflow.

far right: The introverted space of the Wanderer's Lodge displaying the rich play of light that results from the relation between roof lights and windows and structural and sculptural elements.

The Wanderer's Lodge is a building for living, studying and contemplating. The building work started in 1981 with the receipt of a donation of metal structural elements and masonry. The primary structure was completed using these materials, and then left until a state grant for research into weathering buildings funded its completion. The research focused on two aspects of the way nature interacts with buildings – luminosity and wind – and the results define the building's envelope of fuselage and slatted shutters. The fuselage is designed to withstand the fluid effects of wind and rain, its form tested in both a wind tunnel and a fluid dynamics lab. The corrosive effect of coastal winds on materials was also part of the research. Experimentation with luminosity resulted in deep reveals, areas of stained glass and slatted shutters, producing a range of light conditions that lies between the semi-darkness of traditional architecture and the excessive light of glass architecture.

Hospedería de la Rosa de los Vientos o Las Celdas
(Compass Card Lodge)

David Luza Building
Workshop, Hospedería de
la Rosa de los Vientos
o Las Celdas (Compass
Card Lodge), Open City,
Ritoque, Chile,
1998

The building consists of a group of single rooms (cells), each for one teaching assistant, and a shared kitchen and bathroom. It is located adjacent to the sports fields where the school hosts sports classes and a special lecture every Wednesday. During these events the communal kitchen becomes a place for refreshment and for cocktails that mark the end of the communal events.

Compass Card Lodge was completed in 1998 to house single people in the Open City. Designed by its first inhabitants, it consists of four individual cells, each containing a bed and a worktable, and a shared bathroom and kitchen/dining zone whose main feature is a long bar extending to the outside terrace. The building has a metal structure covered by panels rendered on both sides.

Designed and built by David Luza in 2006, this is the only hanging structure within the Open City. The construction consists of reinforced-concrete pylons driven into the sand dunes that support timber columns and trusses.

All other elements – floors, roof, ceilings and walls – hang from this primary structure so that the building does not impact or interfere with the dunes over which it hovers.

Hospedería Colgante o del Taller de Obras
(Hanging Lodge)

David Luza, Hospedería Colgante o del Taller de Obras (Hanging Lodge), Open City, Ritoque, Chile, 2006

Close-ups of the Hanging Lodge.

The Hanging Lodge in the coastal dune landscape of the Open City. The piles and frame for further expansion of the scheme are already in place. The project, like many others, is designed to be altered and extended over time, thus relinquishing the notion of a building as a complete object and finite operation.

A School of Thought: Experimentation and Realisation

The work of e[ad] has raised national and international interest. It stands alone in offering a unique conception of architecture, a corresponding didactic model and its realisation in the Open City. As such it constitutes the clearest example of a 'school of thought' committed to the search for both a local and experimental architecture. In the last couple of decades, Chilean architecture has experienced a renaissance spearheaded by an internationally acknowledged young generation of architects,[3] and it is generally recognised that e(ad) has played an important part in this. What is appealing about the continual search for embodied work is the perpetual redefinition of what the architecture of the Open City might be, instead of seeking to cement an image and identity in time. The question of the local thus becomes an ongoing agenda and process driven by the will to continue to pursue local architecture that is specific to its evolving setting and the community. ᗌ

Notes
1. Our understanding of e[ad] derives from David Jolly having been a student and teacher there for more than 30 years, from his book *La Capital Poética de América: Relación Poesia Arquitectura*, Lambert Academic Publishing (Saarbrücken), 2012, and from the following publications: Godofredo Iommi and Alberto Cruz, *Amereida Poesia y Arquitectura*, Ediciones ARQ (Santiago), 1992; Rodrigo Pérez de Arce and F Pérez Oyarzún, *Escuela de Valparaíso: Ciudad Abierta*, Tanais Ediciones (Madrid), 2003; and Ann M Pendleton-Jullian, *The Road That is Not a Road*, MIT Press (Boston, MA), 1996.
2. Jolly, *La Capital Poética de América*, op cit, p 127.
3. See, for example, a good survey of contemporary Chilean architecture: Tomás Andreu and Claudia Pertuzé, *Blanca Montaña: Arquitectura reciente en Chile*, Ediciones Puro Chile (Santiago), 2011.

Rural Studio

Incarnations of a Design-and-Build Programme

Rural Studio,
Joanne's House,
20K House
Product Line

Faunsdale,
Marengo
County,
Alabama,
2011

The tenth of the 20K House series, which challenges students to design and build a model home that can be rolled out at scale by a contractor for US$20,000; the highest realistic mortgage a person on Social Security could maintain. In this house a square design minimises the perimeter wall area and maximises square footage.

Michael Hensel

Catering for the needs of an impoverished rural community in Alabama through its design-and-build activities, Rural Studio leads the way internationally as a university-affiliated architecture programme with a social remit. Guest-Editor **Michael Hensel** describes how the initiative has grown and developed since it was first established over two decades ago, in 1993, by Samuel Mockbee for students from Auburn University. The realisation of tens of houses and community projects have not only helped to reshape the local environment, but with the more recent strategic approach advanced under Andrew Frear's directorship more long-term projects have been launched and greater emphasis has been placed on the responsible local sourcing of materials, energy and food.

The best way to make real architecture is by letting a building evolve out of the culture and the place. These small projects designed by students at the studio remind us what it means to have an American architecture without pretense. —Samuel Mockbee, in *Rural Studio: Samuel Mockbee and an Architecture of Decency*, 2002[1]

If architecture is going to inspire community, or stimulate the status quo in making responsible environmental and social structural changes now and in the future, it will take what I call the 'subversive leadership' of academicians and practitioners to remind the student of architecture that theory and practice are not only interwoven with one's culture but with the responsibility of shaping the environment, of breaking up social complacency, and challenging the power of the status quo. —Samuel Mockbee, 'The Rural Studio', *ᗭ The Everyday and Architecture*, June 1998[2]

In 1993 American architects Samuel 'Sambo' Mockbee and Dennis 'DK' Ruth cofounded Rural Studio at Auburn University in Alabama. Rural Studio combines third- and fifth-year undergraduate studios as well as an architectural outreach programme that all focus on social responsibility coupled with design-and-build activities to cater for the underserved population and its communities in Hale County. The town of Newbern, where Rural Studio has its home base of administrative facilities, student accommodation, design studio, mock-up yard, wood shop and farm, is situated some 235 kilometres (145 miles) from the university.

Located in the Black Belt region of West Alabama, Hale County has a modest population of 15,406 people with more than a quarter of its citizens living below the poverty line.[3] Most of the county is unindustrialised and remains rural and agricultural. Between 1993 and the end of 2001, Rural Studio completed nearly 50 projects across Hale County, some of which are located in the county's capital Greensboro, the hamlet of Mason's Bend and the studio's hometown of Newbern. Diagnosed with leukaemia in 1998, Mockbee succumbed to the disease in 2001.

Samuel Mockbee's unfortunate death at the age of 57 could well have implied the end of Rural Studio; yet its success and Auburn University's sustained efforts in keeping the studio going resulted in the appointment of a new British-born director, Andrew Freear, in 2002.

Rural Studio,
Harris (Butterfly) House,
Mason's Bend, Hale County,
Alabama, 1997

top: Anderson and Ora Lee Harris on the porch of the Butterfly House.

Rural Studio,
Mason's Bend Community Center,
Mason's Bend, Hale County,
Alabama, 2000

bottom: The glass facade consists of recycled car windscreens.

The work of Rural Studio can be chiefly grouped into client houses, community projects and, more recently, the Rural Studio Farm. In their steady accumulation these projects have begun to reshape the communities in which they are located. In the second incarnation of the studio under Freear's leadership, some locations and themes have emerged as the focus of more developed strategical thinking and long-term planning. Thus, in parallel to continuing along the track established by Mockbee, new types of projects have begun to take shape, such as the accumulative landscape projects at Perry Lakes Park in Marion, Perry County (2005); Lions Park in Greensboro (2006–) and the designs for Talladega National Forest (2008–), as well as research such as the ongoing 20K House project, which derives its name from the maximum realistic mortgage a person receiving median Social Security checks can maintain.[4] In addition, Rural Studio remains outward- and forward-looking in its approach, re-envisioning its own facilities into a self-efficient productive farm charged with producing 75 per cent of its own food.

Houses

From the outset, Rural Studio designed and fixed up or built houses for people whose existence is poised well below the poverty line, starting with the house for Shepard and Alberta Bryant in Mason's Bend (Bryant Haybale House, 1995). Among the best-known examples of the early house projects are that for Anderson and Ora Lee Harris (Harris/Butterfly House, 1996), also located in Mason's Bend. These projects demonstrate a direct engagement with specific individuals and families whose needs are addressed with architecture that does not simply consist of the necessary provisions, but instead delivers interesting and often iconic designs consisting of strong expressive forms constructed from affordable and varied materials. In so doing, architectural design transcends its common existence as a commodity for the rich and becomes a routine enrichment of the built environment.

Rural Studio,
Supershed and Pods,
Morrisette House,
Newbern,
Hale County,
Alabama,
2001

top: The student cottages, or 'pods', are tucked under the canopy of the Supershed.

bottom: The cardboard pod with walls made from bales consisting of reused corrugated and wax-impregnated cardboard strips.

The buildings' local expression comes as no surprise given Samuel Mockbee's origin (fifth-generation Mississippian) and interest in and research into the local architecture of the rural South. While the houses commenced in one way or another as one-off projects, they nevertheless also began to constitute a larger accumulative project. This acquired a clear framework with the development of the 20K House in 2005, which represented a logical progression of Mockbee's work. The Rose Lee House, built in 2008, was the last single-family dwelling before the 20K House project took over the studio's housing research, leading to the expansion of the research-related 20K Project by way of the 20K House Product Line.

The latter includes a variety of activities such as code reviews, as well as need, placement and evaluation criteria and methods for completing model homes. These undertakings deliver coordinated overarching agendas that include observation and analysis of the pattern of inhabitation of individual clients, maintaining the emphasis on meeting occupiers' needs in a manner that is true to the projects of Rural Studio's first incarnation. This is a compelling demonstration that such programmes can ground site and client specificity.

Community Projects
Community projects have been part of Rural Studio's design-and-build

activities from the outset, starting in 1995 with the Yancey Tire Chapel. This was followed by a string of projects including a town hall, and community, senior, children's and learning centres, boys' and girls' clubs, a housing resource centre, library, museums, galleries, farmers' markets, fire stations, an amphitheatre, churches, cafés, bathhouses, pavilions, park facilities, playgrounds and sport courts, skate parks, wheelchair ramps and animal shelters, as well as numerous fix-ups of existing community projects, constituting a portfolio that any architectural practice could be proud of in terms of range, quality and local sensitivity of the work.

One of the most iconic community projects is the Mason's Bend Community Center (2000). The centre is an open sheltered space consisting of rammed-earth walls, and a lightweight metal structure that holds a metal-clad roof and a partial roof and corner clad in reused car windscreens installed in an overlapping fish-scale manner. Another project that stands out is the Newbern Fire Station (2004), the first public building to be built in the studio's hometown in 110 years. The building consists of a timber structure clad internally with wood. The outside is clothed with a standing-seam metal roof and translucent polycarbonate sheets mitigated with a cedar sunscreen facing south. The building itself is not insulated, but utilises

Rural Studio,
Newbern Fire Station,
Newbern, Hale County,
Alabama, 2004

left: Front view of the fire station.

right: The thermal mass of the concrete floor slab, which is exposed to the low-angle winter sun, serves to warm up the interior to prevent freezing of the water in the fire trucks.

passive strategies for shading during the summer and for thermal gain in winter. The fire station, because of its local success, recently received a new civic neighbour, creating a new public heart for Newbern in the form of a Town Hall built of 8x8 cypress timbers. The range of civic projects undertaken by Rural Studio demonstrates the applicability of their design approach to a broad pallet of programmes and small- to medium-scale buildings.

Accumulative Projects
Two accumulative projects stand out in the landscape- and sports activities-related works of Rural Studio: those at Perry Lakes Park and Lions Park. At Perry Lakes Park in Perry County, Alabama, the studio designed and built the Perry Lakes Park Pavilion (2002) and Perry Lakes Park Restrooms (2003) including the 'Tower Toilet', 'Long Toilet' and 'Mound Toilet', all bound together by an elevated walkway, as well as the Covered Bridge (2004) and Birding Tower and Elevated

Rural Studio,
20K Houses,
Greensboro,
Hale County,
Alabama,
2008

top: Northward Development
Houses. Left: Pattern Book
House; centre: Loft House; right:
Roundwood House.

Rural Studio,
Rose Lee House,
Footwash,
Alabama,
2008

bottom: Built by the Second Year Studio, this
20K House is a rift on the expandable house: a
house type that is based on local farmhouses
and is built with the potential to expand and
develop over time, according to the needs of the
occupants and their family.

Walkway (2005). The projects are characterised in the main by low ground impact, light structures and spaces, and careful integration into the landscape of the park. In contrast, at Lions Park in Greensboro, they focused on providing much-needed sports and leisure activities for young people in the town by designing and building the Lions Park Baseball Fields (2006), Restrooms and Surfaces (2007), Skatepark and Concessions stand (2009), Playscape (2010), and Scout Hut and 'park in the park' (2012). In these works Rural Studio demonstrates its capacity to work with projects that evolve over time.

Rural Studio Home
While designing and building for the community, Rural Studio has also continued to develop its own facilities at the Morrisette House in Newbern. One of its most iconic projects is that of the live–work Supershed and Pods (2001). This project consists of cabins where the third-year students lodge. While each accommodation features its own individual design, all are aligned under the Supershed, a roof that provides for sheltered workspace. One of the best-known cabins is the Cardboard Pod (2001), the walls of which are made from bales of recycled corrugated and wax-impregnated cardboard. Most recently, under the leadership of third-year professor Elena Barthel, the studio started to establish its own farm, challenging itself to eat and grow organically and to be 75 per cent self-efficient in the production of its own food ('efficient' suggests an open

The projects are characterised in the main by low ground impact, light structures and spaces, and careful integration into the landscape of the park.

Rural Studio, Perry Lakes Park Restrooms, Marion, Perry County, Alabama, 2005

top: Phase 2 – 2003. Left: tower toilet; centre: long toilet; right: mound toilet.

Rural Studio, Dave's House, 20K House Product Line, Newbern, Hale County, Alabama, 2009

bottom: The eighth of the 20K Houses learns from previous houses in the series. It develops the 'shotgun house' type, which has a single large room with front and back porches. Features of the house have been refined, so that it has a larger front porch in white pine and greater privacy in the interior space.

system allowing barter and exchange while 'sufficient' suggests a closed system that does not engage with its surroundings or community). The farm aims to demonstrate sustainable farming techniques and includes a kitchen garden (2008), commercial kitchen (2010), solar greenhouses (2010–) and workshop facilities. It is through projects like this that Rural Studio opens its own campus to the community and community services.

Postscript
In 2004 Samuel Mockbee posthumously received the Gold Medal of the American Institute of Architects (AIA). This award was well earned by Mockbee, not only for his sustained community-oriented architectural efforts, but also in

generating a momentum in the activities of Rural Studio that could survive his demise, a community in which the relay can be passed on and the race can continue.

Under the 13-year leadership of Andrew Freear with well over 150 projects located in the Hale, Perry and Marengo counties of Alabama's Black Belt, Rural Studio has made and continues to make a considerable difference at the local scale, its wide range of projects having significant impact on the quality of life and accessibility of dedicated design in rural Alabama.

With more than 600 alumni across the globe, the success of Rural Studio can be seen in the number of

similar programmes that have emerged elsewhere, a trend that will hopefully continue with the further development of Rural Studio giving new impetus. While Mockbee espoused a hands-on approach to architectural education and made a clarion call for architects to become social activists, under Freear the studio continues to move with the issues of the day and is now addressing the critical issue of the responsible use of resources: materials, energy and food. ᴅ

Notes
1. Samuel Mockbee quoted in Andrea Oppenheimer and Timothy Hursley, *Rural Studio: Samuel Mockbee and an Architecture of Decency*, Princeton Architectural Press (New York), 2002, p 2.
2. Samuel Mockbee, 'The Rural Studio', in Jeremy Till and Sarah Wigglesworth (eds), ᴅ *The Everyday and Architecture*, July/August (no 4), 1998.
3. United Status Census Bureau State & County QuickFacts: http://quickfacts.census.gov/qfd/states/01/01065.html.
4. www.ruralstudio.org/programs/20k-house-product-line.

Rural Studio,
Newbern Town Hall,
Newbern,
Hale County,
Alabama,
2011

This building provides the town of Newbern, where Rural Studio is located, with an internal community space and also a civic space by creating a wall for a public courtyard along with the previously built Fire Station.

Michael Hensel and
Christian Hermansen Cordua

Scarcity and Creativity
Studio (SCL),
Floating Compression Canopy,
Nusfjord, Lofoten, Norway,
2013

The canopy and the landscape furniture
seen from the fjord approach to the
harbour and main pier.

An initiative spearheaded by Michael Hensel, Christian Hermansen Cordua and Solveig Sandness at the Oslo School of Architecture and Design (AHO), the Scarcity and Creativity Studio (SCL) has been set up with the explicit intention of enabling students 'to learn from integrated design, research and hands-on building activities'. Here Guest-Editors **Michael Hensel and Christian Hermansen Cordua** describe the ambitions and scope of the programme, and the projects that the studio has undertaken at extreme southern and northern latitudes, whether in Chile or in Northern Norway, highlighting the importance of climatic and environmental factors in a local setting.

The Scarcity and Creativity Studio

The Scarcity and Creativity Studio (SCL) at the Oslo School of Architecture and Design (AHO) emerged out of a specific convergence of aspirations, convictions and opportunities. Founded in 2012, the studio pursues the goal of realising works in a climate of experimentation so as to enable students to learn from integrated design, research and hands-on building activities. This is based on the understanding that studios in most schools of architecture are omitting crucial aspects of the architectural process, and in so doing reinforce the chasm between education, research and practice.

SCL's first conviction is that architecture realises itself in buildings. One can 'think' architecture, 'speculate' architecture, 'research' architecture, 'represent' architecture and 'simulate' architecture – and all of these contribute to the studio's understanding. Yet, the full experience of architecture is only realisable in buildings and their inhabitation. The second conviction is that the resistance that materials place between architectural intentions and the capacity to realise them can only be fully comprehended in the building process. Third, architecture is made through the participation of a network of actors – clients, engineers, consultants, authorities, builders, suppliers, researchers – which is a vital reality of the architectural process. Fourth, risk-taking experimentation and research are the principal means to new knowledge, which advances architecture.

The first opportunity that emerged for SCL, and a rather prominent one at that, was an invitation to build at the Open City in Ritoque, Chile. The Open City is a site of experimental architecture run by the School of Architecture and Design of the Pontifical Catholic University of Valparaíso, which has been building there for more than 30 years. Here, strategic finance from the Research Centre of Architecture and Tectonics (RCAT) made it possible for SCL to build three small constructions. Projects have since followed in Lofoten, Oslo and Nes in Norway, and Pumanque in Central Chile, with further projects in Norway and Spain in the planning.

SCL aims to provide students with as full an experience of the architectural process as possible within the context of a school of architecture. This didactic mode is valuable in terms of both the simulation of architectural practice, and taking advantage of the academic setting to allow for research by design that seeks to extend the boundaries of architecture. The projects engage real clients with a need for building, from which a series of constraints emerge: strictly limited budgets, and design and construction time, planning and building regulations and local conditions to be addressed. Once the programme is established with the client, the design

process is run like an architectural competition, commencing with each student developing individual ideas. Through successive project reviews, the number of projects is reduced while the design teams working on each one become larger. At the end of the process, the studio, with the client, chooses the design(s) to be built. Typically projects are designed and constructed within one semester with a construction time of one month.

As part of its agenda the studio attempts to address the problematic between global homogenisation of architectures and building elements on the one hand, and designs that are particular to the specific latitudes and locations of the different contexts on the other. It does so by working with generic building materials obtained from local suppliers and employing the skills of local craftsmen to develop architectures that are specific responses to local terrain, climate, architectural context, needs and, wherever possible, patterns of habitation. The following projects highlight this approach.

Scarcity and Creativity Studio (SCL), Las Piedras del Cielo, Open City, Ritoque, Chile, 2012

An enclosed volume set within the landscape platform of the project provides food preparation facilities.

LATITUDE 33 SOUTH OPEN CITY, RITOQUE, CHILE

In 2012, SCL designed and constructed three projects for the Open City in Ritoque, itself a seminal showcase of architectural and tectonic experimentation and research. The Walk the Line project, set within the coastal dune landscape, provides minimal temporary accommodation for visiting scholars. Hospedería de las Alas is a bird observation shelter placed at the peak of a dune overlooking a river estuary and bird sanctuary, and Las Piedras del Cielo is an outdoor space for communal eating and nature observation, with a small kitchen for food preparation. The projects engage with the objective of the Open City to develop architectures that are particular to South America and, more specifically, to the local Pacific coastal landscape. They experiment with different structural systems that can cope with the impact of the severe coastal winter storms and earthquakes, but with minimum ground impact.

Las Piedras del Cielo is situated next to the wetlands of the river estuary. It consists of a landscaped deck with an enclosed space for a small kitchen, and a textile membrane canopy. The deck provides a sitting surface that forms a horseshoe in plan with a fireplace at its centre. Both deck and canopy are structurally integrated and require only small point foundations, although each foundation is subjected to different and often combined load cases including wind and earthquake impact. The provision for communal outdoor eating combined with nature observation is a reflection of the communal lunch – an important weekly event in the Open City. It aims to externalise this event, giving it a less formal setting within the context and language of the local landscape.

33

LATITUDE 68 NORTH
NUSFJORD,
LOFOTEN, NORWAY

Scarcity and Creativity
Studio (SCL),
2x2 Bathing Platform,
Nusfjord, Lofoten, Norway,
2013

The bathing platform facing the
Westfjord. The project represents
the studio's further development of
screen walls and surfaces for use in
cold climates.

In 2013 the studio designed and constructed two projects north of the Arctic Circle in Nusfjord, a historical Norwegian fishing village with a natural harbour set within the rocky shoreline of the Lofoten archipelago. The Floating Compression Canopy and accompanying landscaped furniture provide an outdoor eating area for Nusfjord's harbour-side restaurant, while the 2x2 Bathing Platform faces the open sea towards the Westfjord. The winter weather of the Northern Atlantic often impacts severely on the local architectures here, and was therefore a crucial design criterion.

The Floating Compression Canopy is located on Nusfjord's main pier facing its natural harbour. It defines the outdoor catering area of the adjacent restaurant that shelters the site to the north. In search of an architecture that makes reference to the boats in the harbour, a tensegrity system was chosen that pays homage to Kenneth Snelson, the inventor of the floating compression system. The materials selected for the canopy – aluminium tubes for the compression members and high-performance rope as the tension element – represent the materials of contemporary boat masts and rigging and, in so doing, blend visually with the vessels that fill the harbour during the warm season.

During the winter, large waves that break on the concrete retaining wall below the pier often lift and damage the pier decking. For this reason, in order to reduce the risk of damage, the decking is not permanently fixed to the substructure of the pier, so panels displaced by the waves can simply be put back. However, this was not possible at the foot-points of the Floating Compression Canopy, where a small area of pier decking needed to be permanently fixed to solve the problem.

The high-performance rope that was chosen for the tensegrity system is frequently used on sailing boats. Splicing, knotting and sewing skills needed to be acquired for this purpose, and in one instance a new type of knot was created. This work falls between craft and assembly, containing elements of both, and offers an interesting instance of skill transfer and modification from one field of application to another. The Floating Compression Canopy thus aimed for a tectonic hybrid between regular and naval architecture. However, over time the rope experienced an unexpectedly large amount of creep, the system lost tension and started sagging, and eventually the structure had to be taken down. Though this could have been avoided by working with steel compression members and cables, the client and design team had made a joint decision at the outset to take this risk.

The 2x2 Bathing Platform, which comprises a sundeck, sauna and hot tub, is located on an undulating granite shore that slopes from the existing buildings that define the northwestern perimeter of the site towards the sea, forming a trough in its centre. Attention to detail was necessary in integrating the project with the existing landscape, focusing also on its capacity to withstand the North Atlantic harsh winter storms and severe waves. A grid of point foundations consisting of steel pins are directly set into the rock to minimise ground impact and preserve the terrain, reflecting a key characteristic of traditional Norwegian architecture. The tectonic of the project is not defined by skilled joining, but instead by a coordinated design and assembly logic that considers the internal seams of the platform wherever it changes in slope, as well as the external edges where it meets the surrounding landscape.

The platform also acts as the enclosure for a transitional semi-sheltered space and the sauna, and in parts is articulated as stepped seating for musical and theatrical events on site during the summer months. The whole is articulated in a screen wall-like manner by alternating the 2-by-2-inch timber profiles with spacers to accomplish visual permeability, rainwater runoff and reduction of uplift. In this project, ground and envelope are indivisible and continuous with the wider landscape.

Scarcity and Creativity Studio (SCL), Floating Compression Canopy, Nusfjord, Lofoten, Norway, 2013

top: Preparation of rope details for the Floating Compression canopy: knotting, splicing and sewing.

bottom: The canopy and landscape furniture on the main pier.

68

LATITUDE
68 NORTH
NUSFJORD
LOFOTEN, NORWAY

68

LATITUDE
68 NORTH
NUSFJORD
LOFOTEN, NORWAY

The bathing platform is set within the
coastal landscape of Nusfjord.

LATITUDE 34 SOUTH
PUMANQUE
CHILE

Scarcity and Creativity
Studio (SCL),
Sørenga Bridge Event
Space,
Oslo, Norway,
2014

The radical transformation being carried out in the eastern part of Oslo city centre left the Sørenga Bridge half demolished. SCL was approached to incorporate the remaining section of the bridge into the leisure facilities the city is building in the areas cleared by redevelopment. The project is a small-scale urban event space and also offers views over Oslo and its surrounding landscape.

In 2014 SCL designed and constructed a new community centre for Pumanque, a town that was devastated by the immense earthquake in 2010. Like Las Piedras del Cielo, the community centre consists of a timber structure and a textile membrane canopy. It comprises two multipurpose rooms, a semi-sheltered transitional space, a roof terrace accessible via a large primary stairwell as well as secondary stairways, and the canopy that partly shelters the roof terrace. The massing of the single-storey building reflects that of those in town: a second floor is a luxury affordable only for a few in Pumanque. The roof terrace thus enables visitors to experience the elevated space of a 'second floor', and takes its inspiration from Villa Malaparte in Capri, designed by Adalberto Libera in 1937. However, while Villa Malaparte has a continuous relation with the rocky outcrop on which it sits, the community centre is instead a mediation between the surrounding buildings and the wider landscape. It reflects the terrain of the hills that flank the town. Yet, unlike the 2x2 Bathing Platform, it does so not as a landform building, but as a clearly defined architectural volume that corresponds with the surrounding buildings.

An exterior screen wall provides for varied semi-sheltered and carefully modulated interior conditions, and is made from 2-by-2-inch profiles using spacers to produce interstices, similar to the 2x2 Bathing Platform in Lofoten. While traditional screen walls are characterised by high-level craftsmanship that results in intricate ornamentation and functionality, such as regulating views, and the impact of heat and light, the community centre screen wall derives its apparent varied articulation from a design strategy based on a simple assembly procedure. The rotation and mirroring of three differently designed panels enables the non-repetitive positioning of six different patterns.

The textile membrane canopy was developed as a re-articulation of the colonnaded walkways that line Pumanque's traditional houses. It provides shading for the spaces adjacent to the community centre building and for portions of the roof terrace, while also reducing the amount of direct sunlight that is let into the interior spaces – a necessary condition at this latitude. The position of the building volume responds to the location of the existing trees, which in conjunction with the building and habitable exterior spatial pockets in the envelope provide sheltered intimate outdoor spaces. The main entrance is centrally located between two interior spaces and sheltered by the screen wall and a bridge that connects the two parts of the roof terrace. This space can serve as an extension to the two interior spaces, combining them into one larger area. The tectonic elements of the project – screen wall, climate envelope and canopy – enter into varied relations with one another and with other space-defining elements such as the trees and the perimeter wall to provide a range of spaces from fully sheltered to exposed and from collective to intimate.

SCHOOL OF THOUGHT

The pursuit that underlies and permeates the work of the Scarcity and Creativity Studio is to develop an approach towards locally specific architectures for different latitudes and parts of the world relative to local circumstances, conditions, cultural patterns and sensibilities. This often entails the realisation of projects using only generic materials that are readily available in nearly every DIY store and low-tech building processes. The limitations posed by the lack of available resources helps focus the design on specific selected criteria such as the production of heterogeneous spaces despite the modest size of the projects, as well as the articulation of specific building elements for different climates – layered envelopes, screen walls and arrayed canopies. In this way, SCL's work is consistent as a 'school of thought' while at the same time seeking to produce difference in response to the particularities of each setting. ⌁

34

LATITUDE
34 SOUTH
PUMANQUE
CHILE

Scarcity and Creativity Studio (SCL), Community centre, Pumanque, Chile, 2014

centre top: The front facade features screen walls and a textile canopy.

middle centre: The articulation of the backyard uses the existing trees.

left: View of the backyard formed by the volume of the community centre, with one of the staircases to the roof terrace on the right.

IN SEARCH OF CONTEXT

Since 1996, **Shin Egashira**, a unit master at the Architectural Association School of Architecture in London, has been leading the Koshirakura Landscape Workshop as part of the AA's Visiting School programme. The village of Koshirakura is in the remote, rural and mountainous region of Niigata on the northwest coast of Honshu, Japan's largest island. Egashira describes some of the projects that have been realised over the years and how they work with the extreme climatic conditions that reveal 'architecture as an art form where frictions between community and climatic forces are inscribed as life expressions on the face of the landscape'.

WORKING WITH
THE FORCE OF ERASURE

During the first weekend of September, in the mountainous area of Niigata, just before the rice harvesting begins, the community of Koshirakura village gathers for the annual Maple Tree Festival, the Momijihiki, a tradition that is believed to be more than 160 years old. During the festival a tree – believed at this time to be inhabited by a god who is being thanked for all blessings – is cut down and carried from the mountain to the shrine for a night of singing and dancing. The main festival begins the following morning when the tree is dragged around the village amongst a lot of drinking, singing, shouting and water fighting. It stops at houses whose occupants have special reasons to offer thanks to the god and who will consequently provide sake for everyone. For the last 18 years the festival has gradually been reinvented with the incorporation of architectural students from around the world into this farming community, where the average age of the villagers is 65. It is this strange and improbable scenario, in which a sense of friction and mixture of ages and languages collaborate, that makes the festival so magical – with the help of the good local sake.

It seems that architecture has increasingly become an object of study with which we learn about the complexity of forces that are constantly influencing the values of and shaping the environment we live in today. Yet we seem to struggle to make sense of the city and landscape that are constantly reshaped by economic, political and cultural forces. As a result we spend much of our time trying to identify various contexts in which architecture can be given new meanings. With this in mind, one cannot help but wonder why there are so many architecture schools in cities where there are already so many architects and buildings, when there are so many places outside cities where architects are needed for their knowledge and tools, not only to improve physical conditions but, more importantly, to read and interpret the inherent qualities of these places.

The work of the Koshirakura Landscape Workshop began in the spring of 1996. The year before that I was approached by the Niigata Prefecture government, who had been trying and failing with traditional approaches to revitalise a community left with an empty school

Shin Egashira/
Koshirakura
Landscape Workshop,
Various projects,
Koshirakura,
Tōkamachi, Niigata,
Japan,
2005

Axonometric views of various projects designed by the Koshirakura Landscape Workshop combined with exploded axonometrics of their constituent parts.

Our objective was to recognise the textures of these landscapes as one side of a coin that had the late 20th-century construction of the city as its other face.

building due to the lack of children. The rejuvenation of post-agricultural communities in rural Japan seemed a challenging agenda for new forms of architectural fieldwork. Back in London, our unit at the Architectural Association (AA) School of Architecture had been working on the theme of (lost) objects in the landscape, looking at a series of post-industrial communities. Our objective was to recognise the textures of these landscapes as one side of a coin that had the late 20th-century construction of the city as its other face. This continual theme reflects one of our current topics: how to represent contemporary cities and landscape by the recursive process of homogenisation? We seek to re-read the city through all the things that are marginalised and fragmented by the forces of economic and political shifts, and find how those erasures often provoke informal public spaces and cultural expressions in the unplanned city, and accidental architecture. In contrast to cities, much tougher forces of erasure are affecting the rural landscape where local industry can no longer sustain the form of its community nor maintain the textural details of its land. In Japan this process started in the 1970s.

Snow, Clay and Rice

When a prevailing wind blows fine sand from mainland Asia across the sea, the moisture-laden air freezes into big snowflakes the instant it reaches the northern edge of the Japanese Alps. This wet and heavy snow accumulates up to a depth of 5 metres (16 feet) by the end of the winter. It is this deep snow that often isolates communities along the mountainside from the rest of the region. Koshirakura is one of 13 villages scattered along the meanders of the Shibumi River that cut deep into the narrow mountain valley made of layers of sand and clay. The instability of this terrain, combined with the steep topography and the force of the snow, continuously reshape the fragile land surface.

Temporality affects the land in Koshirakura in three specific ways: the slow process of land formation; the seasonal cycle of farming; and the rapid change in the price of rice. As a result, the landscape reveals the traces of repetitive patterns of cultivation, the topography and textural details of which emerge and submerge within the forces of nature and the shifting economy of the region's agriculture. Terraced rice fields run along the valleys. Traditionally the cultivation of the land entailed a continuous struggle with the river, snow, earthquakes and landslides. The Niigata earthquake of

Maple Tree Festival, Koshirakura, Tōkamachi, Niigata, Japan, 1999

Koshirakura villagers and students of the Koshirakura Landscape Workshop participating in the annual Maple Tree Festival.

Traditionally the cultivation of the land entailed a continuous struggle with the river, snow, earthquakes and landslides.

2004 devastated many of the villages here. Koshirakura's population is now smaller than 100, a third of what it was 35 years ago.

For 18 years now, the Koshirakura Landscape Workshop has taken the AA architecture school outside of its academic context, stripping off all the usual criteria and siting it directly in the places where architectural knowledge and spatial sensitivities are needed. In return, material experiments have become possible as the rural environment has fewer restrictions for buildings. Yet the extreme climate, both natural and economic, challenges us to exercise our ability to re-imagine spaces with limited resources. It could be this extreme climate that makes architecture an art form where frictions between community and climatic forces are inscribed as life expressions on the face of the landscape. The Koshirakura Landscape Workshop therefore focuses on the reading of the landscape; its representation, from details to materials, allowing a reinterpretation of reality from different viewpoints; and the rearranging of these details into new forms of spatial construction. Intercultural exchange plays an important part in the workshop as participants are accepted as residents of the village, having in turn to accept the duties that come with this.

Shin Egashira/ Koshirakura Landscape Workshop, Cinema screen, Koshirakura, Tōkamachi, Niigata, Japan, 2004

below: During the festival period the screen doubles up as a gate to a shrine.

bottom: Night view of the screen with projection.

Azumaya

'Azumaya' (summer pavilion, or arbour) means archetype of the traditional garden hut – a refuge from the sun and the rain, yet ensuring a free flow of air, water and energy. In 1998, the then Kawanishi town hall asked for the design of a new Azumaya and the project went out to tender. By its nature, it required the transgression of several conventions: the construction process was to involve a collaboration between the Koshirakura Landscape Workshop and the chosen contractor; and apart from the basic structure, several design details would be left 'open' to allow for adjustment during the workshop. The contractor would have to agree not only to work within the timescale of the workshop, but also to be legally responsible for its timely completion. As a result, only one contractor tendered for such a demanding yet so small construction.

The workshop in 1999 included 16 students from the AA and four students of architecture and fine art from Japanese universities who had to learn how to construct traditional timber joints from the chief carpenter. The spatial characteristics of Koshirakura's Azumaya were composed of textures, the roof angles and other attendant details learned from vernacular traditions for dealing with snow. Such features achieve their unique spatial significances as the

Shin Egashira/Koshirakura Landscape Workshop, Azumaya, Koshirakura, Tōkamachi, Niigata, Japan, 1999

both above: Views of the Azumaya in its closed and open states.

below: Villagers taking a rest from cutting grass in the garden surrounding the Azumaya.

The contractor would have to agree not only to work within the timescale of the workshop, but also to be legally responsible for its timely completion. As a result, only one contractor tendered for such a demanding yet so small construction.

Shin Egashira/
Koshirakura Landscape
Workshop, Bus
shelter, Koshirakura,
Tōkamachi, Niigata,
Japan,
1997

above top: The bus shelter
buried under snow in winter.

above bottom: The design
team occupying the
completed structure.

seasons change. A space required for snow clearance inside the structure is used by children for sleepovers during the summer. The movement of the leaves of an adjacent row of blossomed cherry trees registers as flickering reflected light inside the Azumaya, penetrating through the north-facing *akaritori* (clerestory) louvres. The apertures can be adjusted. So too can a sliding bench, and a screen can be reconfigured to allow for activities such as karaoke parties and tea ceremonies. When the sliding benches are drawn in to enclose the structure, the space is smaller and more intimate.

Temporary Roof for 200

The challenge of the 2002 workshop was the construction of a temporary roof for 200 people for the Maple Tree Festival using 'surplus' timber – offcuts from the local timber industry and thinned wood from forest maintenance. The initial framework was formed of eight *nemagari* trunks – the lower parts of trees growing on slopes that are bent from the weight of sliding snow in the winter. The secondary layer was composed of offcut timber from sawmills, mostly end pieces of planks with incomplete rectangular sections. Applying the principle of gridshell structures, we bundled several offcuts together with ropes and extended them into a series of strips 20 to 30 metres (65 to 100 feet) long.

Shin Egashira/
Koshirakura Landscape
Workshop, Roof for
200, Koshirakura,
Tōkamachi, Niigata,
Japan,
2002

above: The temporary Roof for
200 under construction.

below: The primary structure
consists of *nemagari* logs that
are clad with timber offcuts
donated by the local sawmill.

The final layer was the skin, which incorporated other types of offcut timber from the mills. Local farmers often use these offcuts as temporary shuttering for the construction of paddy-field irrigation.

Pizza Oven

The theme of food has always been central to the Koshirakura Landscape Workshop, and in 2011 we incorporated this into our agenda. Next to a 300-year-old cherry tree at the corner of the school entrance, a prime location for the festival celebrations and village community events, we set to build a communal-size wood-burning oven, a rather rare artefact in rural Japan where pizza is normally bought at a restaurant or frozen from the supermarket.

A truck full of sandstone, concrete blocks and *oyaishi* sand stones brought the materials we used to make the lower compartment to be used as firewood storage. On top, a 15-centimetre (6-inch) thick concrete slab was cast to support the oval footprint of the oven. This was composed of materials found locally: 300 kilograms (660 pounds) of clay, 400 kilograms (880 pounds) of sand, and a mix of 50 kilograms (110 pounds) of lime and cement plus a large pile of dry rice-straw surplus. An A-frame timber structure serves as the house for the oven, its shuttering designed to protect it from rain and snow.

Shin Egashira/Koshirakura Landscape Workshop, Pizza oven, Koshirakura, Tōkamachi, Niigata, Japan, 2011

The completed oven, ready for a pizza-baking workshop with the Koshirakura villagers.

Making beautiful buildings or improving the facilities are not the answer to the forces of erasure; however, we have chosen to continue with the Koshirakura Landscape Workshop in the same way that a maple tree for the harvesting festival is cut and replanted every year to be dragged around the village once again.

Fifty pizzas, sweet potatoes, pumpkins, a large fish and a roast beef were successfully cooked in the oven and enjoyed during the Momijihiki festival. Over the next few days we held a pizza-making workshop for the attentive locals, who came with notebooks to gather the exact recipe of the dough and were stricken when we had no precise instructions. Despite this, they practised and studied pizza making, and a few months later, having mastered the technique, opened a popup restaurant serving 200 pizzas to visitors from other villages during the Jimankai event they hosted in November.

A Continuous Event

The village does not need new buildings – it needs residents. Koshirakura is not an exception – its situation and depopulation issues are common throughout rural Japan. Making beautiful buildings or improving the facilities are not the answer to the forces of erasure; however, we have chosen to continue with the Koshirakura Landscape Workshop in the same way that a maple tree for the harvesting festival is cut and replanted every year to be dragged around the village once again. We continue to build, modify, remake and rebuild, seeing the making of architecture as a continuous event; one that might not change the economic forces, but that accepts them and uses them precisely because they provide a creative freedom not possible in other educational or professional contexts. △

Detoured Installations

The Policies and Architecture of the Norwegian National Tourist Routes Project

Since its inception in 1994, the Norwegian National Tourist Routes Project has become a flagship for Nordic architecture worldwide, showcasing installations by local practices along a network of historic tourist roads. The former Rector and Professor of Urbanism and Landscape at the Oslo School of Architecture and Design (AHO), **Karl Otto Ellefsen**, explains how the initiative has adeptly tapped into sustainability trends 'with its emphasis on untouched nature and local authenticity', while also strategically providing a tool for realising wider social, economic and political aims.

Hardangervidda National Tourist Route

The Hardangervidda National Tourist Route passes the largest high mountain plateau in Northern Europe, and was one of the pilot projects of the National Tourist Routes initiative in the 1990s.

The policies of the Norwegian National Tourist Routes project have gained wide international interest. The hundred or so projects and installations that have so far come out of the initiative have been extensively published in architectural magazines all over the world and include works by, among others, Carl-Viggo Hølmebakk, Jarmund/Vigsnæs, Jensen & Skodvin, 3RW and Peter Zumthor. In terms of publication and acclaim the project is the biggest success so far for Norwegian architecture. As an economic initiative it is obviously well timed, catering to a tourist industry that more than ever is looking for thrilling experiences and trips that may be marketed as individually planned expeditions. At the same time it responds to the wider cultural trend of sustainability with its emphasis on untouched nature and local authenticity.[1] The National Tourist Routes project can thus be interpreted as a political initiative with clearly defined intentions and claims on societal relevance and economic output. In the tradition of developing national policies for architecture, it represents a contemporary way of looking upon architecture as a tool for pursuing societal goals. This central policy is put into practice through the use of what was at the start, in international terms, an under-publicised tradition within Nordic architecture sometimes referred to as the 'Oslo School' (see below). The National Tourist Routes project developed into a breeding ground for the renewal of different aspects of this tradition, framed within the most spectacular parts of the Norwegian landscape.

The National Tourist Routes are a collage of 18 historic roads leading through what in terms of tourism are the most appreciated parts of the Norwegian landscape: the western fjords, the midnight sun-lit coastlines and the far north. Some of the routes (like the winding road up Trollstigen and the Geiranger passage) were also originally built for the wealthy international, mostly English, travellers who initiated the fjord-, mountain- and salmon-fishing-based tourism in the late 19th century. Most, however, are pieces of infrastructural engineering constructed to establish land-based connections between towns and rural areas along the coast, and to connect the western part of Norway to the east through mountainous terrain.

Due to the distribution of natural resources in the country, the structure of industries, challenging geography, hydropower, and oil- and gas-based national fortune, Norway has been able to operate both a generous welfare distribution policy and an ambitious regional policy. Most of its rural settlements are still inhabited and relatively prosperous. A fine-grained infrastructure is maintained and the quality of the landscape experience results from a combination of the barren and wild natural scenery and an elaborately cultivated agricultural setting. Although often compared in marketing terms to the competing landscapes of New Zealand and Alaska, this 'alpine' combination of nature and habitat is relatively unique to Norway.

A pilot project was developed and tested from 1994 onwards, and by 1997 four roads had been implemented as National Tourist Routes: following the Hardanger fjord in the west, along the coast of Helgeland up north, in addition to two spectacular mountain crossings over Sognefjell and Strynefjell. Launched as a national policy in 2004, the project has now been set up to span a 20-year period; some 120 of the 200 planned installations are already built. The amount of public money invested yearly is around 15 million euros. The total expenditure at the end of the period will be equivalent to the cost of one prestigious national project such as the Oslo Opera House (2007).

Carl-Viggo Hølmebakk	Sognefjell National Tourist Route
Sight Apparatus	1997
Jotunheimen, Leirdalen	

The architect has installed platforms at three key points along the highest part of this road that indicate optimal lookout positions. The platforms adapt to different landscape situations and are reached via stairs, bridges and pathways. Foundation walls, cast on site, adapt the platforms to the local topography.

Jarmund/Vigsnæs and Grindaker

Tourist facilities

Steinsdalsfossen waterfall near Norheimsund

Hardanger National Tourist Route

2014

The project consists of a parking area with tourist information and toilet facilities in addition to a footpath leading to the 50-metre (160-foot) high waterfall. The elaboration of the access to the Steinsdalsfossen waterfall was the focus of a number of competitions and debate for nearly a decade before its completion.

Sverre Fehn

Nordic Pavilion

Venice Architecture Biennale

1962

Fehn gained international recognition in the 1960s when he produced two of his best-known buildings: the Nordic Pavilion at the Venice Architecture Biennale and the Hedmark Museum in Hamar, Norway (1967–79).

Architecture is currently a part of different kinds of governmental strategies and policies in Europe. The rise of Dutch architecture was linked to governmental policies, France has developed systems for strengthening the role of the architect in transformation processes, and the Danish government supports architectural consultancy as an export industry through a regularly revised strategy. In these initiatives, architecture is primarily a means and not a goal in itself. The discipline is attractive due to the fact that it embodies the potential to handle environmental contexts in a creative manner. Architecture is expected to contribute to solving problems, to display ways to understand complex situations, and to generate ideas.

When the Norwegian Public Roads Administration, after some years of testing, finally initiated the project and selected the 18 National Tourist Routes in 2004, the first and main argument was based on regional policies. The project was supposed to create activity in rural areas for local building contractors, and to create jobs in maintenance, management and support. It was also seen as a comprehensive initiative to develop the tourist industries at a local level. The historic character of the roads was to be cultivated and much effort put into raising the quality of the supporting infrastructure to make them more attractive.

To deliver the quality expected, the National Tourist Routes project established a management system that is highly centralised and top-down. Architects are involved in two different ways: as practising architects designing their own projects, or as representatives of the commissioner. The intention is to raise a profound discussion on architectural quality in every project. In fact, these discussions have been very decisive, resulting in the extension of time allowed for each architectural project, in encouraging conceptual changes, and also in quite a few projects being rejected. The standard required has proven to be rather high.

Most importantly, however, the project has established a system for commissioning architects that gives priority to the young and talented. By cutting their teeth on the National Tourist Routes projects, a whole generation of architects has been exposed to a unique professional experience that has offered them a distinct opportunity.[2]

Wenche Selmer, Summerhouse,

Hellersøya, 1965

Intimately related to the rocky landscape and the sea, the weather-beaten boards are carefully scribed around curves of the rock at the water's edge – a piece of Oslo School iconography.

Architecture is expected to contribute to solving problems, to display ways to understand complex situations, and to generate ideas.

The Oslo School tradition came to be the framework within which the Norwegian National Tourist Routes policies and organisation operate. It was available, had the capacity, possessed a semantic for discussing architecture in relation to nature (as opposed to the built urban fabric), and consisted of the most talented of a generation of architects educated in the 1980s and onwards. It involves both a conceptual modernistic way of working as taught by Sverre Fehn, and the regionally based handicraft and architectural language taught by the architect Knut Knutsen. To denote the tradition as the 'Oslo School' is disputable, as quite a number of the architects designing the National Tourist Routes projects are not linked to Oslo or the Oslo School of Architecture and Design (AHO). The characteristics of this approach to architectural design involve practitioners and academics with quite different backgrounds. However, those who established the tradition – Fehn, Knutsen, Are Vesterlid, Wenche Selmer and Odd Østbye – were all professors at AHO. The tradition was both refined and expanded through their students. And this generation of Norwegian architects constitute both a majority of professors at AHO and of the commissioned architects in the National Tourist Routes project.

The Oslo School architecture is predominantly developed through small-scale projects like single-family houses and cottages, the relation between building and natural landscape is always negotiated as a basis for the projects, and a relatively specific language in tectonics and the use of materials is continually refined. It has furnished the National Tourist Routes project with a quality imbued with certain characteristics. Architecture is profoundly conceptualised as an art form with a relative autonomy. A project is equivalent to an artifice, linked to authorship and part of an artistic tradition where objects are ranked according to their integrity as works of architecture. These works of art are to be considered as a set of unique edifices – exceptional, not to be reiterated or even relocated. The singularity of each project stems from the site-specific character, the conceptualisation of the programme and the creative process of the author. To acquire a full knowledge and aesthetic appreciation, the qualities of the projects have to be experienced contextually on site.

These small *immobilia* along the National Tourist Routes link to an established practice of commissioning architects to design buildings and architectural artefacts based on small-scale and ordinary commonplace programmes. This dates back to a time when architects stood at the front end of creating Norway's welfare-state environments.

Manthey Kula

Akkarvik Roadside Restrooms

Akkarvikodden, Moskenes

Lofoten National Tourist Route

2009

Part of a landscape project by Landskapsfabrikken (Inge Dahlman), the restrooms lie along the European route that connects the string of Lofoten Islands from the mainland and west to the tip of Moskenes far out in the Atlantic. The old toilet facility had been lifted off its footing by strong winds and the new structure needed to be solid and durable. It is thus made of 10- to 12-millimetre ($^3/_8$- to $^1/_2$-inch) sheets of Corten steel welded together on site. Two large glass openings provide views to the sky and the reflected horizon.

The National Tourist Route project responds to the wider cultural trend of sustainability with its emphasis on untouched nature. This hide illustrates the simplicity of most of the programmes. It provides shelter from the elements and a base for the observation of as many as 100 different bird species.

The new piece of architecture, containing a waiting room and toilet facilities, is placed in a humdrum setting, the intention being to cater for pragmatic needs as well as upgrading the character of the ferry station area. In terms of space, materials and details, the project is mainly about experimenting with natural light, transparency and translucency, a concern for a building located close to the Arctic Circle where there are long dark winters and light summers.

3RW Arkitekter

Viewing platform

Ørnesvingen

Geirangerfjorden

Geiranger-Trollstigen National
Tourist Route

2005

Located on one of the many bends along
the winding road running up to the steep
mountains that define the Geirangerfjord,
the platform gives tourists breathtaking
views over this recently designated
UNESCO World Heritage site. The steep
landscape setting and abundance of visitors
to the site in season were challenging and
decisive factors in the design.

Inge Dahlman/Landskapsfabrikken

Picnic area and viewing platform

Kleivodden

Andøya National Tourist Route

2013

Kleivodden is located north on the island of Andøya,
halfway between Andenes and Bleik, and offers a
majestic view of the wide ocean, of the Northern
Lights in winter and the midnight sun during
summer. The platform adapts to its natural setting,
with furniture made from polished Lødingen granite.

The projects are site-specific and nearly all are situated in natural and cultural landscapes.

Although the tradition is today rather frail, the oil wealth of the country combined with generous regional policies has allowed it to survive also in remote areas.

The needs that the National Tourist Routes projects have to cater for, such as view points, paths, rest areas and toilet facilities, are profoundly uncomplicated and, pragmatically speaking, easy to understand. However, the initiative was turned into an arena for cultivating the ordinary and converting down-to-earth programmes into a poetics of architecture – a deliberate approach inherited from the Oslo School mode of working.

The phenomenologically inspired architectural historian and theorist Christian Norberg-Schulz conceptualised 'programme' and 'functionality' by the simple term 'use' ('bruk' in Norwegian), and thereby attached social, cultural and artistic meaning to these concepts.[3] For the Venice Architecture Biennale of 2014, curator Rem Koolhaas chose the title 'Fundamentals' to catalogue the history of dealing with the basic functional elements of architecture.[4] And Christopher Alexander's Structuralist concept of 'patterns', describing the relationship between architecture and socio-cultural phenomena, attempted to discuss the same basics.[5] A poetic and fundamental approach to functionality is readable in the infrastructural projects along the National Tourist Routes, such as the architectonically structured shelters in rest areas, the intricately constructed road fills, and avalanche and snowdrift protection conceived as Land Art.

The projects are site-specific and nearly all are situated in natural and cultural landscapes. Some have emerged from within the existing built environment, but as part of the infrastructural road system, while others relate to a territorial or heritage-based building culture. However, it is the landscape that is predominant in Oslo School discourse. There is a certain complexity and even contradiction in the relation between architectural form and the concept of landscape. Fehn is quoted to have stated 'I hate nature'. If the quote is not only to be considered as a show-off statement, his point is probably that while nature produces its own geologically and biologically grounded aesthetics, architecture follows the grammar of built culture. In Fehn's projects, such as the Nordic Pavilion at the Venice Architecture Biennale of 1962, these two different logics contradict, adapt to each other and overlap. Generally this way of contrasting natural landscape is characteristic of most of the landscape interventions along the National Tourist Routes and most significantly in the projects that celebrate 'the view' with bold installations directing tourists' attention.

70°N arkitektur

Torvdalshalsen rest area

Vestvågøy

Lofoten National Tourist Route

2005

Situated on a bend in the road that is no longer used, the rest area offers spectacular views over the wild ocean and the Lofoten Mountains in the west, and the serene farmland of Borg in the south. It can accommodate several bus-loads of people. A long wooden wall gives shelter from the prevailing wind and separates the rest area from the parking.

This road-level platform with roadside parking celebrates the place from which the painter Harald Sohlberg (1869–1935) did his studies for his most famous work, *Winter Night in the Mountains,* an iconic work of the Norwegian romantic landscape tradition.

In the Oslo School tradition, what suggests itself is to extract the architecture from the site by establishing a constructive geometry that refers to site-specific conditions. This might be handled in an expressive and even ornamental way, celebrating nature by means of architecture and certainly not advancing low-key intentions.

The attraction and focus of landscape tourism along Norway's west coast has always been the romantic notion of conquering the steep hostile mountain slopes and, on reaching the top, taking in the breathtaking panorama of the fjord. The landscape has been ritually monumentalised in certain chosen and adapted sites, and this romantic view persists along the contemporary National Tourist Routes, exhibited in iconic and expressive architectural interventions. Site specificity is also part of this architectural tradition. The distinct qualities and demanding terrain tempt architects to test out site specificity as an option for establishing architectural form by carrying out detailed explorations. Inspiration might come from the established history of a site with the aesthetic experience of the project being intentionally flavoured by historical narratives. Fact-finding and scrutinised investigation of the local is also a means to establish projects that substitute the romantic notion of landscape as something 'out there' with a bodily and intellectual experience of the ecosystem on site.

In the Oslo School tradition, what suggests itself is to extract the architecture from the site by establishing a constructive geometry that refers to site-specific conditions. This might be handled in an expressive and even ornamental way, celebrating nature by means of architecture and certainly not advancing low-key intentions.

Tectonics is an essence – the moral being that architectural form should be constituted by the chosen structure. Most of the projects along the National Tourist Routes display a scale and programme that might be satisfied by joining a few sticks beautifully together. The iconography of the projects is often directly linked to the chosen mode of building construction and to Norwegian traditions of using and handling building materials. The country boasts an unbroken tradition in the use of wood from the times of Viking ships and medieval stave churches, and from the beginning of the 20th century this has been fertilised and refined through the discipline of architecture, via experimentation as well as linking architecture to producers and building industries. Wood in combination with stone, concrete, masonry and steel constitutes both a basic semantic and a vast resource of projects that perform the role of precedents.

Jensen & Skodvin Architects

Gudbrandsjuvet, Valldalen

Geiranger-Trollstigen National Tourist Route

2007

Gudbrandsjuvet is one of the most visited sites along the National Tourist Routes. The intention of bringing people close to the gorge and the cascading water without causing wear and tear to the vegetation and terrain resulted in a design that incorporates suspended footbridges and safety railings. The constructive geometry refers to site-specific conditions and the architecture is constituted by the tectonics of the structure. The project investigates the local landscape and substitutes the notion of landscape as something 'out there' with both a bodily and intellectual experience of the ecosystem on site.

The hotel consists of an old rehabilitated farm with added freestanding individual rooms and facilities. The new modest buildings were set within their forest and riverside locations without modifying the local landscape or ecosystems. Each of the rooms has one or two glass walls that make the forest and river seem part of the interior, and the rugged topography means that each has an individual layout. The project celebrates the notion of being in a natural environment at the same time as underlining the complexity – and even contradiction – of the relation between architectural form and the concept of landscape.

opposite: A collaboration between Zumthor and the artist Louise Bourgeois, the memorial comprises two separate buildings and artworks in memory of the 17th-century Finnmark Witchcraft Trials. Zumthor's installation is accommodated in a long wooden structure framing a fabric cocoon made of a fibreglass membrane. The building that houses Bourgeois's installation is a square structure fabricated from weathering steel and tinted glass. Zumthor is the only architect outside Norway to have so far taken part in the National Tourist Route project.

The National Tourist Routes organisation gives space for the conceptual development of projects by allocating a high proportion of overall costs for the creative first phase.

he National Tourist Routes organisation gives space for the onceptual development of projects by allocating a high proportion f overall costs for the creative first phase. Its policy is to accept rchitectural authorship, and the integrity of authors' development f ideas. It does not represent a revival of the role of the master uilder; it was set up as a discursive, evaluating and negotiating body. he architecture is very much ideas-based. However, it has to be egitimised by disentangling the situation, discussing alternative ideas vith the professionals on the project, and negotiating solutions. Even eter Zumthor in his two projects along the routes has submitted to his process.

Generally the National Tourist Routes project, both politically nd professionally, has been evaluated as a success. However, the programmes for the installations have been criticised for being oo traditional and romantic, not taking consistently into account a contemporary concept of landscape. The notion of architectural quality n the project has been claimed to be too narrow, and there have been accusations that those selected for being both young and talented in he 1990s are now established, and some claim cemented. The critique s met by attempts to open up the discussion on quality, and to recruit new generation of talent for future Routes projects, proposing other deas of landscape, construction and materials.

A more profound critique of the project relates to its meaning. The intention of supporting the tourist industries with public investment is fully understandable, but questions have been raised as to why traditional car-, bus- or cruise-based tourism to iconic landscape situations should be given priority. This critique is also linked to the actual meaning of introducing high-quality architecture in these settings. Could this be looked upon as some kind of environmental pollution of authenticity? These views of the project miss some very essential points. Firstly, the natural attractions are magnets and both the increasing traffic and its impact on the environment have to be controlled. Secondly, pragmatically speaking the installations are needed if rural tourism is to be promoted, and supporting the infrastructure and negotiating with the local landscape by means of the best architecture Norway is able to produce seems to be a most laudable intention. Delivering architectural quality and nurturing new talent are not so easily criticised. ∆

Notes
1. See www.nasjonaleturistveger.no/en.
2. Karl Otto Ellefsen, 'Architecture and Design: Added Value Along Tourist Routes', in Nina Berre (ed), *DETOUR,* Norsk Form/National Tourist Routes in Norway (Oslo/Lillehammer), 2006.
3. Christian Norberg-Schulz, *Stedskunst,* Gyldendal (Oslo), 1995, pp 23–39.
4. www.labiennale.org/en/architecture/exhibition/koolhaas/.
5. Christopher Alexander, *A Pattern Language: Towns, Buildings, Construction,* Oxford University Press (Oxford), 1977.

Conviction Into Tectonics

Christian Hermansen Cordua

The Work of Rintala Eggertsson

Rintala Eggertsson, VOID,
Nordic Pavilion, Venice
Architecture Biennale,
2012

The installation is a comment on society's uneasiness emanating from the fear of the void, which is overcome through consumption that satisfies capitalism's constant need for growth.

*Guest-Editor **Christian Hermansen Cordua** describes how the work of Norwegian practice Rintala Eggertsson Architects is informed by the principals' strong socio-cultural convictions. They believe that raw capitalism alone cannot create a positive environment, as it renders the landscape no more than a site of mechanised production in which as little as possible is invested with a view to gaining as much as possible in the shortest time possible.*

The tectonic richness in the buildings of Rintala Eggertsson Architects[1] resides in the sensory memories the architects evoke and in their capacity to recall deeply stored atmospheres. Sami Rintala says: 'I believe that we're all gathering a sort of memory bank of atmospheres when we are children. I believe that as architects and artists, one of our tasks is to revisit this memory bank and to take these common memories and serve them to other people as atmospheres in their works.'[2]

What is less immediately evident is that their work springs from their preoccupations with our current social condition and their lamentations over what we have made of our world: 'A critical issue for myself is that I do not think that advanced, modern or contemporary culture is such a great thing always – sometimes it is extremely stupid compared to primitive things. To me the word "primitive" can be extremely positive, it can contain so much more information which is so much more necessary information … and primeval meaning, something which is uncorrupted by civilisation, which is an interesting idea, so civilisation can do good things if we are civilised, but it also can corrupt, and can collapse if it does not follow nature.'[3]

Echoing Jean-Jacques Rousseau (1712–78), Rintala Eggertsson outline stages of societal development, but whereas Rousseau does so on the basis of morality, Rintala Eggertsson use the relation of humans to their landscape. Like Rousseau they condemn the last, contemporary stage because it 'turns the landscape into a mechanised system of production, traffic and information simultaneously losing control of it'. The reason for this is that 'our capitalist faith, leads us to accept – as the natural starting point for any productive activity – the idea that you should invest as little as possible and gain as much as possible as soon as possible. … Raw capitalism cannot – and will not – create good environment.'[4]

It comes as little surprise that these convictions have influenced the type of work these architects do.

'My architectural activity so far,' says Rintala, 'has been marginal. There haven't been constructors or even clients asking for it. It has been a kind of research for myself and for the people who have been interested, and so far it has been cultural institutions. So I've had to travel around to get these pieces of work from the people that have been interested in realizing something using my ideas.'[5]

'We have to go far to do meaningful work because we can't do it in the midst of our own problems, we can't see them, there is no problem in our society, sort of, and we don't need to have any answers either. So in our society architects are decorators of the modern vocabulary.'[6]

The work that most clearly expresses Rintala Eggertsson's critique of capitalist consumer society is their VOID installation, which was part of the Nordic Pavilion exhibition at the 2012 Venice Architecture Biennale. In Western tradition, 'void' is usually associated with a lack, a space where something is missing, and with emptiness. In current society's relentless pursuit of progress, voids are things to be filled. The uneasiness that springs from the fear of the void is filled through the consumption of goods, media, entertainment etc and employed as a necessary drive in capitalism's constant need for growth. Exhibiting the void is Rintala Eggertsson's way of exposing their critique of Western society's current conditions. However, they are not primarily critics, but have a deep faith in architecture's potential to help us out of the problems posed by advanced capitalism.

Rintala Eggertsson,
Hotel Kirkenes,
Kirkenes, Norway,
2005

top left : The 'smallest hotel in the world' seeks
to provide a simple refuge for the seamen,
fishermen, hunters, hikers and fortune-seekers
flowing through Kirkenes.

'Parallel to this activism, on the societal level, we should minimise our mass production, mass information and mass traffic to bare necessity. In time, this would result on an individual level in gaining more knowledge and control over one's own environment, production and consumption of local goods and to living with cleverer, smaller and more adjustable infrastructure and architecture,'[7] says Rintala. Two further projects embody these convictions.

The BoxHome, installed at the ROM for kunst og arkitektur gallery, Oslo, in 2007, is a prototype house that Rintala Eggertsson see as a demonstration of how we should live – 'with few possessions and a small space around us'. It alludes to the disappearing Nordic tradition that each family build their own home. Scandinavia is not the only cultural reference; inspired by the Korean way of cooking while you eat, the kitchen/dining table includes two hotplates. Measuring just 2 x 5 x 5 metres (6.5 x 16 x 16 feet), its internal planes, mostly horizontal, semi-divide the volume into four zones for socialising, eating, sleeping and bathing. These are stacked and connected by a steep ladder, every space emerging from and running into another. The outside is clad in aluminium panels while the inside is lined in inexpensive darkly stained cypress boards. The blond wood furniture stands out in contrast to the dark walls.

centre left : With two rooms and a lobby, a total of 27 square metres (290 square feet) and no utilities, the hotel is an appeal to life devoid of unnecessary consumption.

bottom left: View of the sea from one of the two hotel rooms.

bottom right: Ritual burning of the hotel to an electronic soundscape composed by Dza, Kirkenes, February 2012.

Rintala Eggertsson,
BoxHome, ROM for kunst og
arkitektur gallery, Oslo,
2007

top left: The BoxHome installation
proposes an alternative way to
live in a small space with minimal
possessions.

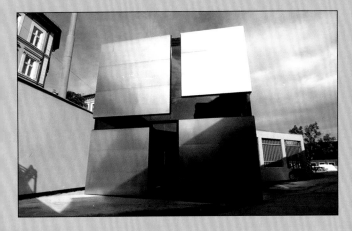

In 2005, a company of art curators and producers called Pikene på Broen invited Rintala Eggertsson to design a temporary project in Kirkenes, northern Norway, as part of the region's Border Dialogues – Barents Art Triennial. Once again, Rintala Eggertsson used the opportunity to highlight their convictions regarding our consumer society. On a site in the town centre facing the sea, on a low budget, and assisted by students and volunteers, they built the 'world's smallest hotel' in 10 days – 27 square metres (290 square feet) with two rooms and a lobby with no electricity or running water. Rintala commented: 'the seamen, the fishermen, hunters, hikers and fortune-seekers flowing through the town need a place to rest that suits their economies, which change like the weather ... All unnecessary luxury would also be eliminated.'[8] Although the hotel gained national and international recognition it was never granted permanent building permission and had to be moved twice. These moves severely affected its condition until it could no longer be used, at which point the architects opted for a ritual burning of the project during which Dza, a leading Russian beat-maker and producer, played an electronic soundscape specially composed for the occasion.

top: Semi-divided into four zones for socialising, eating, sleeping and bathing, every space emerges from and merges into another.

right: All spaces take on multiple uses. The table on the lower level is used for meetings and incorporates hotplates for cooking whilst eating.

top: Waterless toilets and bio-digesters generate methane gas that is used for cooking, and fertilisers used for food production. Solar panels provide electricity while direct solar radiation heats the collected rainwater.

Gardening and crafting are important in Rintala Eggertsson's thinking about architecture as they highlight their unwanted opposites: agriculture and mass building. They see in these two activities the opportunity to learn from and act in sympathy with the local and its traditions. They are not against technological progress per se, but write that 'its exclusive pursuit since the Industrial Revolution has tended to exclude other means of creating assets', which they describe as a 'creative collage of the existing [resources], a collage where the product is more than the sum of its components. Gardening and architecture are examples of this kind of montage.'[9]

Rintala Eggertsson's conviction in the wisdom of local cultures can be seen in the many projects they have designed and built with local communities around the world. One such is the Hut to Hut prototype, organised by the Panchabhuta Conservation Foundation in 2012 as a reaction to growing concerns regarding the impact of commercial tourism on the local environment. Located in Kumta, Karnataka, on the western side of India, it is part of the 1,600-kilometre (990-mile) long Western Ghats mountain range that is home to one of the world's 10 biodiversity hotspots. The objective of the project is to promote eco-tourism, benefiting the area while allowing visitors to experience a unique environment.

The project was developed as a three-week workshop with presentations, discussions and exchanges between participants. The design emerged in the first week and was built by the participants over weeks two and three. The building uses renewable and local materials. Waterless toilets and bio-digesters generate methane gas used for cooking, and fertilisers used in the surrounding gardens for food production. Solar panels charge the interior's LED lighting while direct solar radiation heats tanks filled with rainwater.

bottom: Hut to Hut is intensely local in its conception and use of native renewable building materials.

One of the main qualities of Rintala Eggertsson's work is its tectonic sensibility,[10] which has been described as 'an architecture which plays on the subtle repository of meaning embedded in the residues of our sensory experiences, no longer confined to the individual sensory apparatus, but to a collective sensuousness which is intrinsically cultural in its meaning'.[11] Another important attribute of their work is a socio-cultural conviction and commitment based on a critique of the present and a vision for a better future. What is remarkable, and unusual in an architectural practice, is the integration of 'thought' and 'action'. Something that does not quite fit the prevailing Cartesian view that privileges the work of the 'head' and separates it from that of the 'hand', reflected in the aphorism 'think before you act'. Rintala Eggertsson's modus operandi is closer to notions put forth in books such as *The Craftsman* by Richard Sennett[12] and *The Thinking Hand* by Juhani Pallasmaa,[13] who argue that certain forms of doing embody ways of thinking. ∆

Notes
1. Rintala Eggertsson Architects is a Norway-based studio founded in 2007 with offices in Oslo and Bodø and run by Sami Rintala, Dagur Eggertsson and Vibeke Jenssen.
2. Sami Rintala, video: http://vimeo.com/24350184.
3. Sami Rintala, Lecture, School of Architecture, Norwegian University of Science and Technology (NTNU), Trondheim, 15 November 2012: www.youtube.com/watch?v=6QTBT1Qr8YE&index=7&list=PLUHTGp7T4Zn8p3c-CEudoc-nj3vZyjkqJ.
4. Rintala Eggertsson, 'From Market to Garden: Planting the Seeds for the Next Civilization', unpublished paper, Bodø, Norway, 2 August 2013.
5. Sami Rintala, video: http://vimeo.com/24350184.
6. Sami Rintala, 'South of North: Lessons for the Future', South of North Helsinki Seminar, 10–12 October 2013. Ten teams of Nordic architects were interviewed on their work in developing environments to produce an exhibition and a series of seminars, part of which can be seen at: www.youtube.com/watch?v=wcsuuocs8G4.

7. *Ibid.*
8. See http://europaconcorsi.com/projects/17835-Rintala-Eggertsson-Architects-Hotel-Kirkenes.
9. Rintala Eggertsson. 'Architecture: the Inhabited Resource', unpublished paper, Bodø, 7 March 2014.
10. I use the term 'tectonic' in the Frampton sense that architecture is as much about structure and construction as it is about spatial experience. See Kenneth Frampton, *Studies in Tectonic Culture: The Poetics of Construction in Nineteenth and Twentieth Century Architecture*, MIT Press (Cambridge, MA), 1995.
11. Mari Hvattum, 'Space and Sensuousness in the Architecture of Sami Rintala', Defining Space conference, University College Dublin, 2008.
12. Richard Sennett, *The Craftsman*, Yale University Press (New Haven), 2008.
13. Juhani Pallasmaa, *The Thinking Hand: Existential and Embodied Wisdom in Architecture*, John Wiley & Sons (Chichester), 2009.

TYIN tegnestue Architects

Integrating On-Site Education and Practice

Founded by Andreas Grøntvedt Gjertsen and Yashar Hanstad, TYIN tegnestue Architects grew out of an initiative to provide sleeping accommodation for an orphanage in Thailand when the principals were only third-year architecture students. Norwegian architect **Lisbet Harboe** explains how the student-architects built up a practice while in schools by refocusing their studies and those of their peers on learning through their own experiences of construction.

YIN tegnestue, Soe Ker Tie
ouse (Butterfly Houses),
oh Bo, Tak, Thailand,
009

pposite: Sleeping units at the
rphanage.

elow: Barbecue and sitting area
etween two of the sleeping units.

right: Bamboo is used in
different ways to create a
variety of wall surfaces for the
sleeping unit interiors. Beds
are built on top of each other to
leave room for other activities
on the ground floor, such as
games and homework.

In August 2008, Andreas Grøntvedt Gjertsen and Yashar Hanstad bid goodbye to the campus at the Norwegian University of Science and Technology (NTNU)) in Trondheim and headed for the jungle in Northern Thailand. They had at that stage completed the first three years of their architectural education and wanted to make a difference. They had a client in Thailand, and took with them the money they had raised and the knowledge of two architecture students. Together with landscape architect Line Ramstad they set themselves the challenge of designing and overseeing the construction of six sleeping units for an orphanage in the village of Noh Bo. The project they built, Soe Ker Tie House (Butterfly Houses), was the catalyst for their practice, TYIN tegnestue. It demonstrates a propensity towards richness in the architecture of the everyday, employing local materials within a sustainable design, and the contributions of skilled and unskilled local workers.

Ingenuity and beauty characterise the firm's use of local materials. The main load-bearing structure of the Butterfly Houses is made of 6-by-1-inch ironwood boards layered and bolted to create a flexible, efficient and elegant solution. However, the architectural students also took responsibility for the entire orphanage site, renovating existing outdoor areas and adding infrastructures such as pipelines and paths. The repairs and new constructions were implemented with the combined pragmatic, sensual and social understanding of place that is characteristic of the work of this young practice. This first project was self-initiated, self-organised and self-funded. At the end of this autumn semester, Gjertsen and Hanstad went back to Trondheim, presenting the work to fellow students, teachers and the examiner, who approved of their work and encouraged them to continue what they had started, despite the ensuing challenges.

Education Through Practice

From here on, Gjertsen and Hanstad took charge of their own education as well as initiating on-site workshops and studios for the university and their fellow students. In January 2009 they prepared a three-week workshop, led by professors Sami Rintala and Hans Skotte, in which 20 students designed and built a communal library house for another orphanage in the area, the Safe Haven Orphanage. Concurrently, Gjertsen and Hanstad designed and led the construction of the Safe Haven Bathhouse at the orphanage. Gjertsen and Hanstad had previously participated in workshops led by Sami Rintala where they had acquired the relevant building experience and on-site design skills they relied on so much during these, their first building projects. Together with three student colleagues,[1] they stayed in Thailand for the whole spring semester, completing the Soe Ker Tie House and the Safe Haven Library and Bathhouse before taking on a third, urban site in the Min Buri neighbourhood of Bangkok.

Gjertsen and Hanstad combined in practice not only design and construction, but also educating themselves – and others – all at the same time. Though they did not drop out of school, they left the university campus for construction sites, making the latter their place of study. They recount how they organised their days and their education on site at Noh Bo:

'A typical day:
Most of the morning is used on the building site for supervision and problem solving, while evenings are spent hanging over a big drawing board under an enormous mosquito net.
A typical week:
Mondays we have planning meetings ...
Wednesdays are study days while Sunday is 'holy'.[2]

TYIN tegnestue, Old
Market Library,
Min Buri, Bangkok,
2009

opposite: Looking into the Old
Market Library and community
house.

left: Backyard space with pergolas
made of recycled materials.
Large ceramic pitchers that had
been left behind on the site were
reused for climbing plants.

below: The interior offers
a colourful but tranquil
atmosphere. The ladder leads
up to a mezzanine floor.

In addition to managing an on-site design and
construction studio, they organised their own theoretical
and case studies in collaboration with Hans Skotte, who
acted as their distant advisor.

Over time, TYIN tegnestue have developed an
architectural expertise in how to design and build
profoundly relevant projects within a short period of
time, using what is to be found locally. Through their on-
site approach they have acquired the same skill set as
architects working with temporary projects in the city,
combining meticulous planning and free improvisation.
They know what has to be planned ahead and what can
be left to process and circumstances. These are the sorts
of developed competencies that can be acquired only
through experience, and seem to provide the architects
with a greater ability to hold on to the prime ideals and
keep shared ideas in sight while remaining open to the
different contributions that are necessary for diverse on-
site participatory processes.

Old Market Library, Min Buri, Bangkok

For the local library community project in Min Buri, Gjertsen
and Hanstad and their three fellow students used their
self-acquired on-site knowledge in collaboration with
Bangkok-based group Community Architects for Shelter and
Environment (CASE). The Min Buri area had deteriorated
from a lively market district to slum-like conditions. The task
was therefore not only to provide built structures, but also to
contribute to a social neighbourhood network that enabled
community engagement, aiming to improve the quality of
the physical and social surroundings and trigger a process of
local empowerment.

Together with CASE and the Min Buri community, the
Norwegian students developed a programme, a project and
a building process for the Old Market Library. Throughout the
whole project, TYIN tegnestue and CASE organised regular
meetings to map needs, plan, discuss solutions and also
clear garbage. When building began and the project became
tangible, many local men became actively involved, working

right: 'TYIN's guide to on-site designing and building, developed by professionals through hands-on experience and field-tested under extreme conditions, includes texts and sketches that offer simple and humorous advice, as well as practical tips on how to proceed with a project with tight schedules, small budgets and limited resources.'

below: View from the atrium of the training centre. The openings in the brick wall hold different types of cinnamon.

bottom: The 600-square-metre (6,460-square-foot) roof surface with the atrium trees rising through the centre of the roof plane.

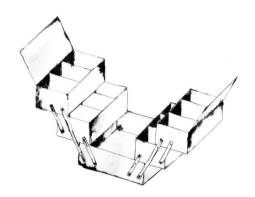

on site every day. The renovation of the old market building into a local library with new structural additions and interiors was carried out using local materials. Wooden platforms, half a metre above the seasonally flooded floors, and a mezzanine floor, were constructed to offer quieter places for reading, study and contemplation. In the backyard, sun-protecting pergolas and greenery establish another kind of tranquillity. Simple but considerate actions reformed the place, making it useful, comfortable and alluring – as a tangible poetry – commonly experienced and enjoyed.

TYIN Architect's Toolbox

There is always an aspect of TYIN tegnestue's architecture that communicates with the visitor, appealing directly to the senses and evoking joy. They are places made of local, inexpensive materials while using simple yet ingenious building techniques, all embedded in the local as tailored solutions. The shifts between different types of stones on

the ground and wooden materials on the walls to make the sunlight shine through in various ways are examples of their sensitive use of materials. It is difficult to imagine such an understanding of architectural material and social performance without the on-site education they pursued.

As Master's students, Gjertsen and Hanstad operated independently of their educational institution, but with advisory support, continuing their theory studies in parallel to their on-site work. Rural Studio, the undergraduate programme at the School of Architecture, Planning and Landscape Architecture at Auburn University in Alabama (see pp 40–47) and Nabeel Hamdi, a pioneer of participatory planning emphasising the value of participatory work in building communities, were important inspirations, providing critical references as the students constantly and persistently discussed and analysed their work and way of operating. They continue to review their performance, technical solutions and architectural forms, looking at local

TYIN tegnestue,
Boathouse, Aure,
Norway,
2011

top left: This coastal house replaces a derelict boathouse on the coast of Møre in western Norway. Though inspired by the placement, form and materials of traditional boathouses used for the storage of vessels and fishing gear, the new house serves mainly recreational purposes.

top right and right: The side wall of the boathouse can be opened up completely by lifting elements of the wall, creating full integration between inside and outside while also extending the roof for rainy days.

Notes

1. The three architecture students were Pasi Aalto, Magnus Stensvåg Henriksen and Erlend Bauck Sole.
2. Yashar Hanstad and Andreas Grøntvedt Gjertsen, *TYIN Noh Bo: Soe Ker Tie House – 2008,* Trondheim, 2008, p 323.
3. 'TYIN Architect's Toolbox': www.TYINtegnestue.no/ arbeider/TYIN-architects- toolbox/#.

social impact and the wider political implications, as well as developing an architectural-pedagogic approach to on-site learning. Their simple and down-to-earth TYIN Architect's Toolbox offers a worldview, a simple and committed response, and a set of tools 'needed to create useful, beautiful and necessary structures in any circumstance'.[3] Their on-site methods and tools have influenced architectural education at NTNU where their office is now situated and where they also teach.

Practice as Architects and Educators

The history of TYIN tegnestue is a story about two architecture students who, during their Master's studies, developed both an architectural practice and an educational approach. By the time they graduated in 2010, TYIN tegnestue had completed four projects under extreme conditions. Their work now includes projects such as the Cassia Co-op Training Centre, in Kerinchi, Indonesia, a 600-square-metre

(6,460-square-foot) facility for cinnamon production, with 100 people working on site in 2011, the Aure Boathouse on the coast of Norway, as well as the Lyset paa Lista (The Light of Lista) workshop at the southernmost tip of Norway in 2013, which included students from Norway and Mexico. In order to fight migration and develop tourism, the workshop at Lista was organised to build a small yet visible visitor centre to attract attention and investors. The clients were 50 local landowners.

Their participatory project Barnetråkk in Oppland, Norway (2013), a playhouse for local children along their route to school, was built by TYIN along with Rintala Eggertsson Architects and students from the Oslo School of Architecture and Design (AHO), with the children themselves involved in the planning process. The Arne Garborgs veg 18 for a single-family home extension in Trondheim, completed in 2014, was one of their first commercial ventures. ⌀

Text © 2015 John Wiley & Sons Ltd. Images: pp 82-5, 86(bl&r), 87 © Photos: Pasi Aalto/pasiaalto.com. Courtesy of TYIN tenestue; p 86(t) © TYIN tegnestue

Peter Buchanan

Renzo Piano

Mobile structure for
Sulphur Extraction

Pomezia, Rome

1966

Lozenge-shaped panels (some of them
translucent) stiffened by a central crease and
downturned edges form both the structure
and cladding of this vaulted shelter that was
moved by dismounting panels at one end
and remounting them at the other – an early
fusion of elegant frugality and straightforward
functionality.

Renzo Piano

Poet of
Technology

The architecture of the Renzo Piano Building Workshop (RPBW) is renowned internationally for the formal refinement of its components and detailing as well as for its sensitive responses to context, both in terms of its physical surroundings and local construction traditions. But, as architectural author and Piano specialist **Peter Buchanan** reminds us, the central concern of the practice remains focused on the original core impetus of expanding the bounds of what technology and materials can achieve.

Reflecting his background and personality, Renzo Piano's architecture is centred on making and experiment, the latter largely exploring technologies of making. Initially narrowly focused, his range of design concerns progressively expanded out from these over the decades. Yet throughout he has been obsessed with pushing materials and construction techniques, old as well as new, to unprecedented extremes, as well as with 'lightness and transparency', his oft-repeated mantra. As we shall see, though, lightness refers to more than mere physical weight, and transparency to more than being able to see through things.

Born into a family of builders in the densely knit industrial and port city of Genoa, a favourite outing during his boyhood in the post-Second World War years was to accompany his contractor father to construction sites. He enjoyed the docks too, particularly watching airborne goods being craned off and onto ships. And he spent happy hours beneath the washing lines on the roof of the family home, using drying sheets as suspended canopies, as delighted by their soft curves as by their sunlit luminosity. The resonances with the architecture to come are obvious.

Renzo Piano

Factory

Genoa, Italy

late 1960s

top: Rooftop view showing how panels rise at their centres to meet a circular plate bolted to the head of the supporting prop below and are creased for stiffness.

bottom: Each square structural bay, defined by slender posts rising from footings sitting directly on the ground, was roofed by 16 panels craned in together with props dangling from their centres to then be secured to a web of tension ties.

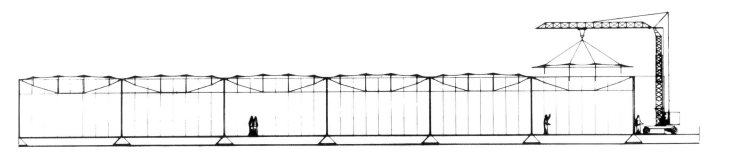

Renzo Piano Building
Workshop (RPBW)

IBM Travelling Pavilion

Rome

1983-6

top: The mobile pavilion was assembled from demountable half-arch trusses, with laminated wood chords and a three-dimensional web of polycarbonate tetrahedral that were pinned at apex and base and abutted at gutters to form an elongated transparent vault whose every component was clearly articulated and displayed.

bottom: The transparency, along with the warmth of all the wood, softened the impact of the modularly faceted forms so that the pavilion settled easily into place in verdant sites against historic buildings, such as here beside the Castel Sant'Angelo in Rome.

Early Works for Industry

Piano was cripplingly shy and insecure as a boy and young man, and had to prove himself privately against objective measures. With his early buildings – industrial shelters commissioned and built by his father during the latter half of the 1960s – he did this by devising structures that spanned a maximum distance or enclosed the largest volume using a minimum weight of materials (objectively measurable criteria) to fulfil another early goal: creating spaces unobstructed by internal supports. With all these he pioneered his characteristic trait of assembling buildings from purpose-made 'pieces' specific to that building and intrinsic to its identity.

Unlike a building, the 'piece' is small enough to be prototyped, tested and progressively refined in form and performance. Some early structures were vaults, and the 'pieces' simple lozenge-shaped panels of materials such as glass fibre whose downturned edges stiffened the panels and allowed them to be simply bolted together. By unbolting those at one end and re-bolting them to the other, the vault could move, as did that at a sulphur extraction works. But some vaults were atypical in Piano's development, with a single 'piece' as both structure and enclosure.

More typical were industrial sheds where the weather-excluding roof panels were propped from a cable suspended between posts. The panels, again of fibreglass, were shaped to both stiffen the thin material and ease the transfer of structural forces between the vertical rods and the horizontal portions of the panels. Separation of structure and enclosure, and the seeming simplicity and refinement of the jointing elements, all heralded Piano's future.

This phase of Piano's career climaxed with the Italian Industry Pavilion at the 1970 Osaka world's fair, a square building framed from steel bars with roof and walls of square polyester panels supported on suspension ties from external masts. The thin panels were again stiffened by their shape and, in what became a Piano trademark, the jointing elements were understatedly elegant. An impressed visitor was Richard Rogers, with whom he formed the architectural partnership (Piano & Rogers, 1971–7) that won the Pompidou Centre competition, launching both to international fame.

Renzo Piano Building
Workshop (RPBW)

The Menil Collection

Houston, Texas

1986

opposite bottom: The over-sailing roof reveals the trusses, assembled from bolted-together units of cast ductile iron, supporting the glass roof propped above them and the ferrocement, light-diffusing blades below them, all of which are above external walls framed in steel I-sections and clad in the same grey clapboarding as the surrounding bungalows in the background.

Renzo Piano

Italian Industry Pavilion

Expo '70

Osaka, Japan

1970

Construction view shows how the structure was assembled from slender I-beams taking compressive forces and tension ties, the latter also bracing the centres of the polyester cladding panels, to create a pavilion of striking material economy.

Piano & Rogers: The Pompidou Centre

Wishing to explore innovative steel structures, engineers Arup paid the architects to design the Pompidou entry. Again it is a clear-span structure, described by engineer Peter Rice as 'a large loose-fit frame where anything could happen'. But instead of a suspension system, the solution consists of huge trusses whose ends bear on gerberettes,[1] bone-like elements pinned to the columns and acting as levers, projecting out to ties tensioned downwards. Thus the vast central spaces are flanked by narrower ones between the columns and ties for circulation and services. Although a mechanistic solution, it is also, as with much Piano design, somewhat Vitalist, with a skeleton of bones and sinew and servicing viscera outside the glazed skin.

The Pompidou (1978) climaxes an architectural era as much as opens a new one. Although a triumph, Piano recognised its limitations, referring to it later as 'a young man's building' and 'an act of loutish bravado'.[2] Needing to rethink and expand his design approach, he entered the most experimental phase of his career in partnership with Rice (Piano & Rice, 1977–81) who remained his key collaborator until Rice's premature death in 1992.

Piano & Rice: Technical and Social Experiment

Piano and Rice shared a creative creed: that the lingering spark of discovery is what people subliminally respond to in works that expand the bounds of technical possibility. Both also sought new potentials in traditional materials and techniques, as well as in pushing newer ones to unprecedented limits or exploiting the latest of these. A key issue was to determine the right balance for each building, place and time between local, traditional materials and leading-edge imported ones. Such concerns, and the resultant broad palette of materials, marked Piano's buildings as very different to conventional High-Tech with its dogmatic commitment to 'the technological imperative' and 'technology transfer'.[3]

Explorations undertaken by Piano & Rice included two prototypical vehicles (1978–80). A car for Fiat had a strong structural frame (the stresses within which were more easily analysable than was usual at the time) with body panels glued to it, an approach now widely used. And a multi-purpose

Renzo Piano Building
Workshop (RPBW)

Beyeler Foundation

Riehen, Switzerland

1997

A crepuscular view of a portion of the
end elevation of the gallery – that first
encountered on approach – reveals
the elements, or 'pieces', from which it
is assembled, yet also, for reasons of
decorum, recalls the porticoed front of
a traditional museum.

vehicle for developing countries had a concrete flat-bed
chassis-cum-load platform to which various configurations
of body panels could be attached along with the mechanical
components. Another project was a set of television
programmes (1979) exploring how historic communities and
craftsmen collaborated using simple tools to erect even such
virtuoso structures as Gothic cathedrals.

Awakening and drawing on a similar collaborative spirit,
a brilliant project from this period was the mobile UNESCO
Neighbourhood Workshop, first deployed in Otranto, Italy, in
1979. UNESCO sought a strategy to conserve whole historic
towns, rather than individual buildings, without displacing the
residents. The approach devised combined the use of high-tech
equipment for accurate surveys of existing conditions along
with simple tools (developed by Piano and Rice) easily usable
by local craftsmen, empowering them rather than rendering
them obsolete. Aerial surveys, for instance, involved towing a
helium balloon with a motor-driven camera slung below. And
in place of standardised industrial components, pipe-bending
equipment was used to tailor-make light trusses to exact size to
prop historic floors and roofs while residents remained in place.

Renzo Piano Building Workshop: Technology and Place

The project that returned what was now the Renzo Piano
Building Workshop (RPBW) to international attention was the
IBM Travelling Pavilion (1983–6). This was a demountable
series of three-pinned arch trusses, with chords of laminated
wood spars and a three-dimensional, weather-excluding 'web'
of polycarbonate pyramids, all connected by supremely elegant
joints of cast aluminium. With its liberal use of wood, including
the sensually shaped spars, this combined elegance and warmth
to great popular acclaim. For Rice, a major headache was
resolving the very different rates of expansion of the various
materials, which he eventually solved (seemingly effortlessly)
with spacer-bolts taking up the movement.

Shortly after, The Menil Collection in Houston (1986)
marked the start of Piano's mature career in combining
technological innovation with respect for local context and

Renzo Piano Building
Workshop (RPBW)

Maison Hermès

Tokyo

2001

bottom: To limit the lateral seismic forces
entering the tall narrow structure, and
so lessen the swaying of the suspended
skin of brittle glass blocks, Arup
engineers borrowed a trick from historic
pagodas, fixing only the central (blue)
columns into the earth and allowing
some damped vertical movement in the
rear (red) columns.

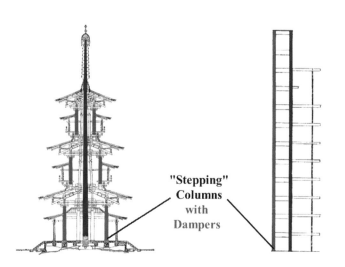

"Stepping"
Columns
with
Dampers

culture. The characteristic 'piece' here is a truss-cum-light-diffusing element. This fuses bone-like components of ductile iron (a material from the auto industry) with shapely sun-excluding and light-diffusing blades of ferrocement (from boat building). These have formal affinities with furniture by Charles and Ray Eames, the supporting steel frame is deliberately derived from buildings by Craig Ellwood, and the cladding is the same grey-painted clapboard as on the surrounding suburban bungalows. The building thus marries the transfer of leading-edge technology with America's two vernacular building traditions: the steel frame and the clapboard-clad balloon frame.

Here the ferrocement blades seem to float on the light flooding through them, proving that for Piano lightness is not just a technicality, but also about aesthetic and empathic responses. In addition, all structural and technical elements are revealed, so the building is transparent in the sense too that it is easily 'read' and understood, and the 'pieces' are purposively shaped to those ends. So, just as materials and forms relate the building to local context along with aspects of American architectural culture generally, lightness and transparency go beyond the display of virtuoso technique to also engage users in terms of aesthetics and comprehension.

Piano later went further, assembling buildings from multiple smaller elements, progressively peeled away to reveal each layer of 'pieces'. With the over-sailing eaves of the Beyeler Foundation museum (1997) in Riehen, Switzerland, 'pieces' drop away until only individual glass panels reach out to float on the air like an eagle's wing-tip feathers. And he continues to push traditional techniques to new extremes, such as the local stone arches (the widest spanning ever) of the Padre Pio Pilgrimage Church (2004) in San Giovanni Rotondo, Puglia, as made technically and economically feasible by the computer – for analysis, precision stone-cutting and checking for invisible flaws.

His hallmark, unparalleled skill at combining innovative technology with local elements, or the evocation of them, is beautifully demonstrated at Maison Hermès in Tokyo (2001). To ride out earthquakes, and inspired by traditional pagodas, only a central column row of the tall, narrow structure is anchored in the ground, and the others can pull free somewhat. Slender interior columns (between ball joints hidden in floor and ceiling) take only axial loads in spaces startlingly similar to those of Japanese tradition. This illusion is reinforced by the shoji screen-like outer skin of huge glass blocks – four times the area of normal ones, and each subtly different (another technical feat). These glass blocks are flexibly sealed to suspension rods so the whole skin ripples slightly during tremors, while at night the whole building shines like a huge Japanese lantern.

Thus Piano remains committed to experiment and innovation, but discerningly so for his ends are evocatively poetic as well as technical. Pointing out a distinction some miss, he is wont to say: 'For me, technology is like a bus; I only get on if it is going in the direction I want.'[4] ∞

The glistening skin of extra-large glass blocks enveloping the flagship luxury goods shop evokes the preciousness of the merchandise inside and also glows at night to resemble a gigantic Japanese lantern.

Notes

1. Named after 19th-century German engineer Heinrich Gerber who invented the beam/cantilever solution for bridges.
2. Peter Buchanan, *Renzo Piano Building Workshop – Complete Works: Volume 1*, Phaidon (London), 1993.

3. Some British architects and writers of the time argued for a creative obligation to use the most advanced materials and techniques (the technological imperative), especially those adapted from other high-tech industries (technology transfer).
4. As remembered by the author.

The Pr
of Mak

Studio Mumbai

Studio Mumbai
workshop,
Mumbai,
2014

The workshop setting is akin to medieval cathedral workshops in which master builders and different specialised craftsmen interact and co-design through scaled and full-scale mock-ups.

Studio Mumbai,
Installation
for the '1:1
Architects
Build Small
Spaces'
exhibition,
V&A, London,
2010

View of the Studio Mumbai workshop with the full-scale mock-up of the V&A installation.

Michael Hensel

Located in a studio space just south of Mumbai in India, Studio Mumbai is closer to a traditional craft workshop than a conventional architects' office. With over 100 carpenters based on site, the studio is able to realise large-scale mock-ups, as well as models and graphic representations. As Guest-Editor **Michael Hensel** explains, craft and the collaboration between craftsmen is at the very core of the practice. Within the workshop typical roles become blurred: as carpenters become architects, architects enter the craft of carpentry; and they both pursue the field of masonry. Out of an affinity for craft comes an empathy with the local, whether expressed in a respect for site and the land or indigenous materials and building traditions.

The medieval cathedral workshops – referred to in German as *Bauhütten*[1] or *Dombauhütten* – were organisations that were made up of craftsmen with the range of skills necessary for the construction of a Gothic cathedral. This consisted not simply of local fraternities of stonemasons – even though they assumed the key role - but, instead, involved all crafts that were permanently required on site, including cathedral master builder(s), foremen, stonemasons, bricklayers, carpenters, blacksmiths, glaziers and so on.

It is interesting to imagine the scene that must have presented itself upon entering a cathedral workshop building, which were in the main made of wood, and to picture the tangle of different activities, conversations, work pieces, workstations and tools.[2] While the cathedral workshop tradition came to an end in 1731 due to their prohibition by Emperor Karl VI, there exist today contemporary cathedral workshops that undertake the large amount of maintenance and restoration required to sustain cathedrals over time. They too offer to the visitor an extraordinary experience with a plethora of work pieces, tools and craft-specific activities.

Clearly Studio Mumbai does not design Gothic cathedrals; yet, walking into the Studio Mumbai workshop evokes an image of how one might imagine a cathedral workshop. Located in Mumbai, as the name of the studio suggests, it consists of a series of small buildings and industrial sheds with transitional areas built from scaffolding elements that are clad with corrugated tin sheet, all arranged around an open courtyard set within a dense stand of trees. Most spaces are open to the exterior courtyard and filled with an extraordinary number and diversity of activities, models, mock-ups, materials, objects, bookshelves, workstations, tools and craftsmanship; about a hundred carpenters work for Studio Mumbai.

This setup immediately conveys the vital role of communication and crafts in the conception of Studio Mumbai's designs. Principal Bijoy Jain states in the firm's biography that the studio 'is a human infrastructure of skilled craftsmen and architects who design and build the work directly … ideas are explored through the production of large-scale mock-ups, models, material studies, sketches and drawings. Projects are developed through careful consideration of place and a practice that draws from traditional skills, local building techniques, materials, and an ingenuity arising from limited resources.'[3] Yet, does the rich scope of knowledge and expertise, and the consolidation of these capabilities, not represent the most vital resource, significantly transcending what governs common practice?

Studio Mumbai,
Leti 360 resort,
Leti,
Uttaranchal,
India,
2007

Impressions of the
material transport
on the narrow
mountain trail.

The biography confirms this by stating that 'the endeavour is to show the genuine possibility in creating buildings that emerge through a process of collective dialogue and face-to-face sharing of knowledge'.[4] The workshop is organised accordingly in such a manner as to facilitate dialogue and exchange between different sets of expertise so that a deep conversational interface is created over time. Carpenters enter the field of architecture, architects the field of carpentry, and together they enter the field of masonry, and so on. The plethora of objects plays an equally vital role. The description of Studio Mumbai's and Michael Anastassiades's *In-Between Architecture* installation at the 2010 Venice Biennale also applies to their actual workshop: 'Our immediate environment is a space that we subconsciously create and inhabit. We can make this space familiar or we can expose ourselves to

unfamiliar elements that provoke our response and reevaluation.'[5] Studio Mumbai's master roofer is a Frenchman by the name of Jean-Marc Moreno, who learned his profession through a school in France called Les Compagnons du Devoir. Monsieur Moreno described this school as 'more like a guild; they are the people who built the cathedrals in Europe in the 11th century',[6] which is where the imaginary circle concerning work space closes.

One of the works designed and built at the workshop was Studio Mumbai's project for the 2010 exhibition '1:1 Architects Build Small Spaces' at the V&A in London. The scheme explored a space between existing buildings between the Studio Mumbai workshop and an adjacent warehouse. In the words of the studio, the project constitutes 'a distilled architectural study of dwelling, a home for multifunctional

spaces consisting of communal living environments, places for refuge, contemplation and worship'.[7] While this is a very small project, it nevertheless had a pivotal role in the foray of Studio Mumbai into the field of masonry construction. This shows how the studio is capable of utilising all opportunities to further their material interests and inquiries, and craft-related expertise.

Located in the foothills of the Himalayas at an altitude of 2,350 metres (7,710 feet) above sea level, the Leti 360 resort (2007) is accessible only on foot by way of mountain trails. The resort consists of a public living/dining pavilion and four small guest buildings, all set within the existing terraced terrain, which is shaped by agricultural use. Farming and grazing of sheep, goats and cattle continue on site and between the buildings. Construction posed a challenge, with the nearest road at a distance of 9 kilometres (5 miles)

View of one of the units and the way it is located on the sloping terraced terrain.

Interior of one of the units.

from the site. All materials that were not directly available on site, such as teak wood, glass, metal sheets, canvas, furniture and solar panels had to be transported by porters and mule. Over 70 local craftspeople, including masons and carpenters, participated in the construction, which therefore had to be planned according to seasonal weather patterns and local customs, halting during the monsoon and winter season. Indigenous construction methods and materials were deployed. The stone used for the dry-stacked walls was locally extracted and configured. A structural frame supports the roofs and is glazed towards the exterior. The architecture is conceived as temporal and designed for a 10-year lifespan, and the buildings are therefore easy to disassemble. The dry walls are already beginning to be colonised by local fauna, enabling the natural and agricultural landscape to reclaim the site.

Studio Mumbai,
Palmyra House,
Nandgaon,
Maharashtra,
India,
2007

The courtyard
during the
monsoon rain.

Studio Mumbai's best-known project is perhaps the Palmyra House in Nandgaon, India (2007). The house is located in a dense coconut grove, and its two volumes are arranged in such a manner as to preserve as many of the existing trees as possible (a feature that also characterises some of their other projects). While the two volumes are made from timber, a stone-paved surface articulates the courtyard, which features palm trees, a pool, a well and water channels. Four wells on site supply water for the house and irrigation of the plants by way of the water channels. The kitchen is located in a small building of its own, separated from the two timber volumes.

The number of models, mock-ups and detail tests that fed into the design of the house are surprising. Moreover, the density of the palm tree stand meant that the entire house was built by Studio Mumbai carpenters without the use of large equipment. The structural parts are made from a local hardwood called ain. Exterior surfaces are made from wood or copper, with interior surfaces in teak wood or cement plaster. The external louvres are made of Palmyra, a local palm species, and act like a screen wall to provide shelter from the elements, and to preserve privacy. The louvre screens facing the pool in the courtyard are floor-to-ceiling folding doors that

Details of the louvre facade.

The courtyard space between the building volumes, towards the pool.

View across the courtyard and the pool between building volumes.

when opened create a continuous interior and exterior, a strategy that is spatially appealing but also enhances ventilation of the shaded 'interior'.

Both volumes of the house feature double-height spaces and a section of the upper floor opens out over these. Glazed surfaces in the envelope are only on the upper floor, closer to the canopy of the palm trees. In this way the tree canopy averts steep-angle light affecting the lower floor, while the interior receives plenty of indirect light.

For the Copper House II in Chondi, India (2011), located in a dense mango tree grove, the initial construction of a well resulted in excess soil that

was used to elevate the base of the house in order to prevent flooding during the monsoon season. The house is organised around a stone-paved courtyard with an open family room and more enclosed spaces facing either the courtyard and the surrounding garden or only the latter. Screen walls line large parts of the lower floor, in some cases as folding doors to allow continuity between exterior and interior space. Again the element of water features prominently with a pool, a well and a stream in the lush garden. Two copper-clad volumes at opposing corners of the rectangular footprint protrude above the roof of the first floor and accommodate the bedrooms. The roofs slant towards

the courtyard to create a veil of monsoon water. Light on the ground floor is modulated via screen walls, fluted glass, the overhanging roof in the courtyard, the coloration of materials, and also the vegetation in the garden, engaging building and garden in a continuous spatial relation.

What characterises the work of Studio Mumbai is their incredible, considered observation of what exists locally, ranging from site features to traditional ways of using the land, and to local materials, crafts and sensibilities. These features are carefully integrated into the designs, which also convey a signature of sorts of the studio. However, this is

View of the interior.

Studio Mumbai, Copper House II, Chondi, Maharashtra, India, 2011

The Copper House and its lush garden surrounding.

The courtyard during the monsoon rain.

One of the louvred spaces of the Copper House.

Notes
1. The word *Bauhütte* was introduced, after their demise, by Johann Wolfgang von Goethe in *Kunst und Alterthum am Rhein und Mayn*, Vol 1, 1816. The Gothic cathedral workshop developed from early medieval workshops consisting of monks and ended de facto in 1731 when Emperor Karl VI prohibited them.
2. Günther Binding, *Baubetrieb im Mittelalter*, Wissenschaftliche Buchgesellschaft (Darmstadt), 1993.
3. *El Croquis 157 – Studio Mumbai 2003–2011,* November 2011, p 4.
4. *Ibid.*
5. *Studio Mumbai: Praxis*, Toto (Japan), 2012, p 194.
6. *Ibid*, p 188.
7. *Ibid*, p 47.

not expressed in idiosyncratic form, but rather in a spatial sensibility and continuity from exterior to interior, in recurrent themes in building elements and materials that are appropriate to site and climate, and in the sensitive integration of design processes and local resources. Each design is so intricately linked with its specific locality that it seems impossible to imagine works by Studio Mumbai for a generic context. True, the installation at the V&A captured some of Studio Mumbai's spatial sensibility in a highly internalised way; by necessity the project needed to create its own locality in an introverted fashion.

But while this could be one way for Studio Mumbai to design projects in a dense urban context, one would imagine that an eventual realised project in such a setting will be surprisingly more complex and sensitive to the more subtle traits of locality. ᗪ

Philip Nobel

The Builder's Name

SHoP and the Ethics of Knowledge Transfer

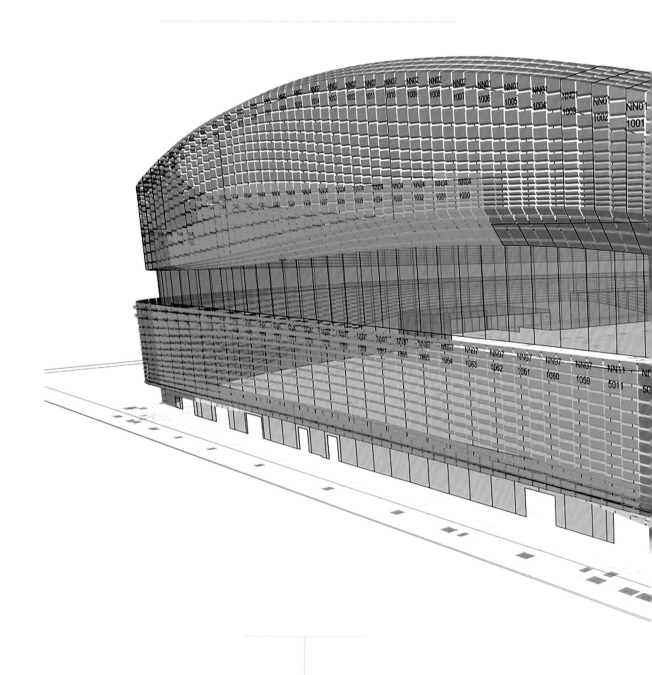

Since its inception in 1996 in New York City, SHoP Architects has fixed its sights on reshaping the relationship between design and construction; not only by pioneering the use of new building and modelling technologies, but by assuming a new level of responsibility for the management and assembly of components. **Philip Nobel**, architectural author and Editorial Director at SHoP, describes how the practice's longstanding engagement with construction has led to an awareness of the importance of the empowerment of builders, leading to responsiveness to local conditions and a proper connection between designers and those who deliver their designs.

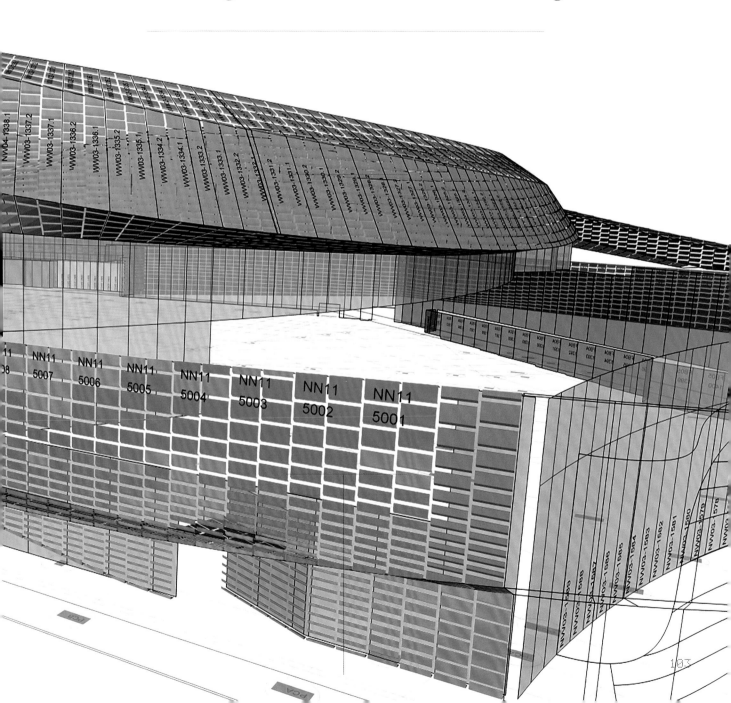

In no art is there closer connection between our delight in the work, and our admiration of the workman's mind, than in architecture, and yet we rarely ask for a builder's name.

— John Ruskin, *The Stones of Venice*, 1851–3[1]

SHoP,
Barclays
Center arena,
Brooklyn,
New York,
2012

previous page:
Each of the 12,000 unique panels of the arena's exterior could be tracked from fabrication through installation with a series of data tools SHoP developed and shared with subcontractors and the client.

right:
Responding minutely to local conditions, the arena has become an icon and an economic driver for the Brooklyn renaissance.

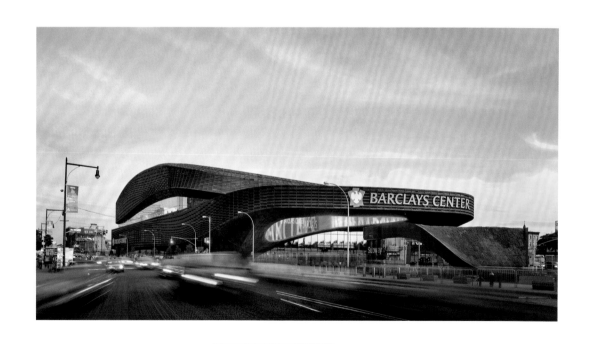

When SHoP Architects began its project to re-imagine the practice of architecture, the firm stated many goals. It wanted to mend a division of roles that has, over centuries of specialisation, introduced a host of technical, and even social, inefficiencies into the process of construction. It wanted to re-establish the design and assembly of buildings as an integrated pursuit. It wanted to reverse the destructive trend, so common among its peers in those early years, of privileging form over use, contemplation over action, the unreal over the realised. Quite simply, SHoP wanted – at that time very much against the tide of convention in academic realms – to build.

Seventeen years on – and 12 since the publication of *Versioning*, the guest-edited issue of this journal in which SHoP laid out many of these goals[2] – the firm has built. Not only its signature projects, but the signature systems that have made them possible. Long before the dawn of building information modelling (BIM), the office was precocious in adopting modelling softwares into the core of its process, pioneering best practices in direct-to-fabrication methods that today are becoming industry standard. By radically streamlining the modes of communication between designer and builder, by assuming the risk of managing the production of components as well as the responsibility for their ordered assembly on site, by putting everyone – suppliers, trades, even clients – literally on the same interlinked and dynamically modelled 'page', SHoP learned to bypass the common bottlenecks that can bedevil construction, weak points in the process of building that can, in aggregate, become a drag on the quality of urban environments at every scale.

This mastery of technology is a clear and today universally acknowledged win for architects, not only for its efficiency, but for the inherent possibilities of imbuing architecture with the complexity it needs to respond minutely to local conditions while achieving its expressive ends. With a tight budget and a crashed timeline, the Barclays Center arena (2012), now an established icon as well as a cultural and economic driver of the ongoing renaissance of Brooklyn, would simply not have been possible to produce by architects working in the old mode: communicating at the speed of redlines, limiting their engagement with construction out of fear and habit, accepting traditional job-site hierarchies, refusing to assert the right of a generalist profession to the generalists' true scope of action.

But having established that new scope, that freedom with and control over the process of construction, other opportunities become available to architects as well. These are perhaps less obvious, but they are no less welcome to a firm that counts among its interests the amelioration of the entire culture of building, not excluding the wellbeing of the people who actually build.

The Workman's Mind

Buildings, it needs to be said in light of our collective enthusiasms for technology, are built by people. By necessity then – moral necessity – an ethical renovation of architectural practice will incorporate an ethical approach to construction work, including sensitivity to local conditions of social want or need. This requires a reconsideration of the established habits of architectural thought commensurate in

SHoP,
Konza Techno
City
Pavilion,
Nairobi,
Kenya,
2013–

Planned for a 2,020-hectare (5,000-acre) site, 60 kilometres (40 miles) outside of Nairobi, the Konza Techno City will be a sustainable technology hub supporting a population of up to 250,000.

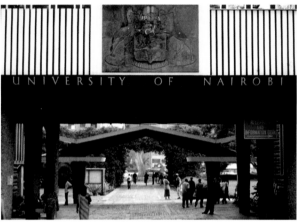

role. In its projects in Africa – the Konza Techno City Pavilion outside of Nairobi (construction of which began in 2013) and the Botswana Innovation Hub in Gaborone (due for completion in 2016) – the transfer of cutting-edge technical knowledge is going hand in hand with the high-tech creation of novel structures.

On a visit to the University of Nairobi, SHoP partner Bill Sharples first identified the possibilities. 'They have a fabrication lab, but it wasn't up to contemporary standards,' he recalled. 'We were meeting with graduate students there, but there was also this 14-year-old kid. We had a conversation with him – of course he was the one who knew everything about the tools they had. We realised this is something we could play a role in: supporting our clients and the local building culture in terms of getting the right software and equipment, teaching the techniques.'[3]

The intention of this ongoing tech-transfer effort goes beyond mere donation, beyond the potential for neo-colonialism that is an obvious risk of that mode of engagement; it is driven by an interest in responsible action and facilitated by the accessibility to shared data made possible by the new modelling technologies themselves. This is particularly apparent in Botswana, where the firm has made an effort to use local fabricators for aspects of the Innovation Hub, a 32,500-square-metre (350,000-square-foot) complex of laboratory research and meeting facilities.

'Our goal was to first set up a classroom with university students who can partake in design development, and then to train local labour,' said Jonathan Mallie, the partner in charge of the firm's embedded construction services enterprise, which is playing a dual role in construction and education in Gaborone. 'There are components, critical aspects of the design, that we are planning to manufacture with local fabricators so they can learn the new methodologies. The government is very interested in this sort of outreach.'[4]

scale to the changes affecting the profession's approach to architectural method, a situational awareness to practice that goes beyond augmenting the landscape to include as well those who people it.

SHoP refined this approach in New York City, where a sense of civic fairness has always driven both its public- and private-sector projects. Working further afield now, the firm has also begun to take on a new, necessary

top and centre: Through an education partnership with the University of Nairobi, engineering students will oversee the fabrication of components for the new structure.

right: The pavilion is the first structure to be built pursuant to a masterplan SHoP has designed for a technology-centric urban development outside of Nairobi.

'There's a thirst for knowledge in Africa,' SHoP partner Chris Sharples added. 'They may be more open to embracing technology there than in any other part of the world.' And with a dynamic model of the project in hand, and a local workforce introduced to its possibilities, ages-old barriers to construction communication collapse. 'You're walking the site with an iPad and you've got the model right there,' Bill Sharples explained.[5] 'Unlike old-fashioned blueprints, a guy with a shovel can understand it immediately and see what it is we're all going to be doing together. It's simple. But it's revolutionary.'

Empowering builders opens up other possibilities, too: the introduction of efficiencies, the improvement of methods and even details during construction in response to local conditions – a mutually beneficial feedback loop between designers and those who make their designs real.

Delight in the Work

The same tools that are allowing an elevated dialogue between designers and builders in Botswana and Kenya – the creative exploitation of Revit and CATIA modelling, as well as the on-site testing of Dassault Systèmes' new 3DExperience platform – can also play a role in making a socially aware architecture possible closer to home. This was true at the Barclays Center, where Mallie credits SHoP's approach to information sharing with changing the quality of interaction on the construction site itself. 'Once that door is open,' he recalled, 'there's the opportunity for positive, collaborative evolution of partnerships that can have a beneficial effect on the design. You begin to influence the culture of building around you.'[6]

At the heart of SHoP's efforts in this area is an abiding respect not only for making, that chic buzzword of our times, but for the people, the men and women, who will do the making. In a recent appearance with the critic Paul Goldberger in New

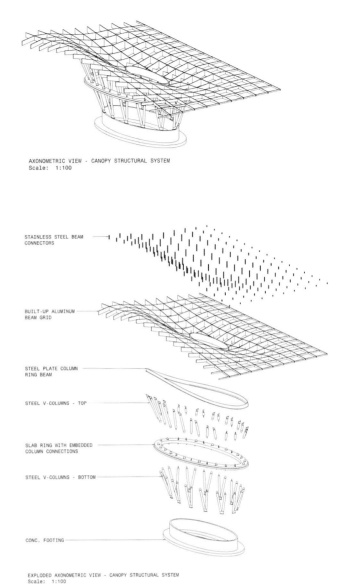

AXONOMETRIC VIEW - CANOPY STRUCTURAL SYSTEM
Scale: 1:100

STAINLESS STEEL BEAM CONNECTORS

BUILT-UP ALUMINUM BEAM GRID

STEEL PLATE COLUMN RING BEAM

STEEL V-COLUMNS - TOP

SLAB RING WITH EMBEDDED COLUMN CONNECTIONS

STEEL V-COLUMNS - BOTTOM

CONC. FOOTING

EXPLODED AXONOMETRIC VIEW - CANOPY STRUCTURAL SYSTEM
Scale: 1:100

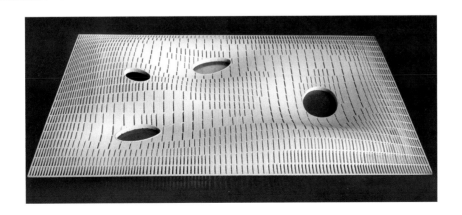

top: The clarity of representation possible with digital design tools fosters much-improved levels of communication on-site between designer and builder.

right: The roof of the partially open-air structure comprises a large number of unique panels to create the required conditions of shading and ventilation.

York, SHoP partner Gregg Pasquarelli has pointed out that: 'Architects don't build buildings – we make instruction sets for other people to build buildings.'[7] There is an inherent respect for the task of building in that formula; a respect for the builder that is evidenced moreover in the firm's efforts to demystify and rationalise those shared 'instructions'.

This process began for SHoP in its first projects, in the simple one-to-one digital printouts used as templates – in the construction of the *Dunescape* installation at the PS1 art centre in Queens in 2000, and in the far more elaborate, but equally accessible assembly diagrams that were given to the contractors working on the structures in SHoP's public park at Greenport, New York, several years later – and it continues in all of the firm's work today. Again, this is at once a creative choice, a business decision and an ethical imperative: a conscious effort to respect those undertaking the act of construction by eliminating the gap, the features of architectural representation that make space for the voodoo and the mystery, the obfuscation and the mendacity, that has for at least a century now separated those who draw from those who build. When that mystery is gone, when everyone on a job site has equal access to knowledge, the traditional and much-defended primacy of architects on the site can be replaced by the creative possibilities, and the profound efficiencies, made possible by conditions of simple, shared, human industry.

At a time when the treatment, the basic safety, of construction workers is often in the news, when atrocities involving exploited labour are increasingly being reported at construction sites in the developing world, this applied humanism has become a distinguishing characteristic of the firm, one its principals seek to underscore. For the conference 'Who Builds Your Architecture?' convened in New York in 2013, SHoP supplied a forceful statement of its beliefs in this regard. It read in part:

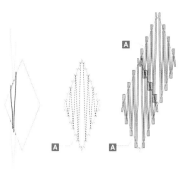

Tiling Method

System Development

The act of creating architecture does not end when the drawings leave our office. The men and women in the field who build our buildings are an extension of our own workforce, who execute, with their skill, care and knowledge, sometimes at the risk of their lives, what we have dreamed and planned and organized. As professionals, we have an ethic that governs the way we conduct our business and treat our employees. We cannot then look the other way if that ethic is violated in the construction stage of our work. Civilized communities cannot be built on the backs of slave labor.[8]

There is more than a hint of the Ruskinian in this stance; in essence it is a contemporary recasting of the social and economic conclusions Ruskin came to via his adulation of the Gothic in *The Stones of Venice* (1851–3) – a book, by the way, that is floating around SHoP's office as a samizdat printout from Project Gutenberg. Ruskin detailed there his understanding of Gothic architecture not as a style – indeed, he despaired of categorising it except as an attitude or a process – but ultimately as no more or less than a humane measure of a worker's free mind. Writing at the advent of the Industrial Revolution, Ruskin railed in his glorious, florid way against the effects of mechanised standardisation on the souls of workers, extending his critique, crucially, to the end user: like contemporary activists promoting the boycott of corporations with questionable human-rights records, he imputed a culpability to all those who use or purchase – or, in the case of architecture, inhabit – the products of a debased culture of craft.

The difference today, of course, the great opportunity, is that the variety that Ruskin sang in the Gothic, the evidence of the freedom of thought, even the imperfection, that he believed could show true loving labour, can, through our new tools, be accommodated into systematised production. But without that necessary feedback loop, the incorporation of the workers' hands and minds in that production, the acceptance of their creative input, their humanity, by the architects, we truly do no more than renew an ages-old misappropriation of labour in modern guise.

Ruskin wrote that in architecture as in any craft, you 'cannot have the finish and the varied form too'.[9] The former, he argued – work made slick by the repression of the workers' will – carried with it the shameful residue of a caged mind, and he believed the immoral burden of that caging would always colour the finished work. The latter state – work that gave evidence of a collective will and that might ennoble those who made and used it – was the humane ideal. Varied, collaborative form was also a signal feature of a quality that Ruskin credited among the very few by which architecture could be fairly judged: virtue. ⌂

Notes

1. John Ruskin, *The Stones of Venice* [1851–3], National Library Association (New York and Chicago), 1905, p 39.
2. SHoP, ⌂ *Versioning: Evolutionary Techniques in Architecture*, September/October (no 5), 2002.
3. Interview with the author.
4. *Ibid*.
5. *Ibid*.
6. *Ibid*.
7. Gregg Pasquarelli, quoted in Sara Polsky, 'How SHoP Became NYC's Go-To Megaproject Architects', *Curbed National*, 28 May 2014: http://curbed.com/archives/2014/05/28/how-shop-became-the-goto-architects-for-nycs-megaprojects.php/.
8. SHoP, 'WBYA 2.0, Who Builds Your Architecture? Part 2: Sustainability and Sustaining Human Life', 29 April 2013: www.shopdoes.com/2013/04/29/wbya-2-0-who-builds-your-architecture-part-2-sustainability-and-sustaining-human-life/.
9. Ruskin, op cit, p 114.

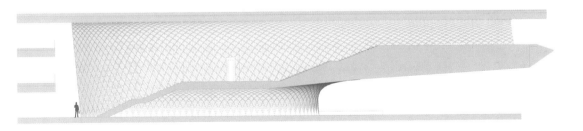

top: The facility includes a data centre and engineering levels, as well as an HIV research laboratory run by the Botswana Ministry of Health in partnership with Baylor, Harvard and Pennsylvania universities.

right: The pattern as applied to the interior spaces of the building's auditorium, where it will also serve as an acoustic baffle.

Søren S Sørensen

Informed
Non–Standard

En Route to
Performative

Twelve years after the 'Architectures Non Standard' exhibition at the Centre Pompidou in Paris, **Søren S Sørensen**, architect and Director of the Advanced Computational Design Laboratory (ACDL) at the Oslo School of Architecture and Design (AHO), argues for a repositioning of the Non-Standard approach. He advocates a performance-orientated method for architecture that can accommodate the evaluation of real-time data sets and environmental simulation techniques in order to assimilate context-specific and climatic conditions, like temperature, wind and humidity, in the design process.

The 'Architectures Non Standard' exhibition initiated a potent discussion in architecture when it opened at the Centre Pompidou in December 2003. The ripples generated by the event, and impact of the related developments since, are striking. The exhibition set a key precedent for the way digital architecture was to be perceived internationally, shifting it out of the exclusively experimental domain into new ways of materialising computer-generated form. Displaying prototypes, experimental and completed projects by 12 international architectural teams, proponents of digital methods and techniques since the early 1990s, the exhibition focused on the capacity of computational design to produce formal results coinciding with changes in the industrialisation of architecture towards a non-standard production. Curated by Frédéric Migayrou it included works by influential offices like UNStudio, Greg Lynn FORM, ONL (Oosterhuis_Lénárd), NOX and Asymptote. Emphasising the capacity of computer-aided design, production and industrialisation, the purpose was to showcase 'the generalization of singularity, in a new order that would be the non standard'.[1] Presupposing changes in design and production tools of architecture based on a widespread use of algorithmic systems, the exhibition also aimed to demonstrate how the architectural profession is being redefined.

The non-standard architectural approach and the potential for further changes in the conception, design and materialisation of architectures is still relevant a decade later, and may be even more so considering the tendency of globalisation processes to propagate standardised components, materials and solutions while disregarding local conditions.

Architectural design and discourse emphasise to a great extent the discrete and finite object, and the discussions emanating from the 'non standard' exhibition, which in essence highlighted the formal potential of what could be seen as idiosyncratic architectures, soon focused on application of technology and became limited to topics on formal exercises, superficiality and the architect as mere programmer or systems designer. Grounded in a fear of unfamiliar technology this is still often the case both within the architectural community and outside, especially when discussing iconic buildings developed through computational design methods. It is therefore important to look closer at what has become of the non-standard architecture approach and the latent potentials that may change the way architectures are designed and materialised.

Positioning Non-Standard Architectures

Branko Kolarevic stated in 2005 that 'the generative role of new digital techniques is accomplished through the designer's simultaneous interpretation and manipulation of a computational construct in a complex discourse that is continuously reconstituting itself'.[2] Positioning non-standard architectures within a framework of performance-oriented architectural design for such data-driven recursive processes integrates evaluative simulation processes and form generation to achieve performance based on data, variations, analysis and optimisation. Integrating context-specific and real-time data sets, for example climatic conditions like temperature, wind and humidity, in the computational data-driven design methods and generative design processes can lead to what can be termed 'informed non-standard' architectures.

Non-standard architectures and the re-emerging role of local, context-specific conditions that may underlie and inform integrated computational design approaches signals a needed shift that emphasises architecture and environment interactions. Quantifiable datasets of local conditions as input in the design process will influence solutions, adaptation to site, use of materials and so on that could benefit sustainability and, in turn, affect building codes and regulations.

The relation between locality and homogeneous globalisation of architecture is by no means new to the architectural discourse, and even though the formal potential has been foregrounded and pursued, non-standard architectures can just as easily be particularised to local conditions as any other architectures, yet facilitate a greater scope of variation in spatial organisation and tectonics.

Kenneth Frampton stated in 'Towards a Critical Regionalism: Six Points for an Architecture of Resistance' that the objective for critical regionalism 'is to mediate the impact for universal civilization with elements derived indirectly from the peculiarities of a particular place'.[3] He argued a governing inspiration could be found in local light qualities or the topography of the given site as well as in structural modes, while cautioning against approaches emphasising optimised technology. Optimisation could limit designs 'either to the manipulation of elements predetermined by the imperatives of production, or to a kind of superficial masking' that could lead to what he called 'high-tech' approaches based only on production and 'the provision of a "compensatory facade" to cover up the harsh realities of this universal system'.[4] In 'Ten Points on an Architecture of Regionalism: A Provisional Polemic' he pointed out that tendencies towards overt optimisation, normative plans and standardised construction methods are 'reducing architecture to the provision of an aesthetic skin'.[5]

Parting from the constraints of normative plans and standardised solutions, non-standard architectures is a first step in addressing this. The primary emphasis must, however, shift from idiosyncratic formal expressions celebrating their superficial differences towards architectures that are intensively embedded into their local environment. A performance-oriented approach pursuing integrated spatial and material strategies to articulate the built environment, to respond to and modulate local climate, can facilitate a broad range of spaces for condition-related patterns of use and habitation.

Layers, Transitions and Local Climate

Contrary to traditional separation between interior and exterior through solid walls and clearly defined openings, the Wall House by FAR frohn&rojas, located in a suburban area outside Santiago de Chile, is based on a series of layers structuring the house, creating a gradual transition between the two and including the exterior in the hierarchy of interior spaces. Completed in 2007, the house is structured around an inner concrete core surrounded by a layer of structural wooden shelving that together with the core defines the primary structure. The climate threshold consists of the final two layers: a primary high-insulation polycarbonate glassed envelope, and a soft fabric membrane acting as an energy screen and protective barrier. Spaces between the wooden structure and the glassed envelope organise the house concentrically into a protected core and surrounding interstitial interior space. An exterior sheltered interstitial space created by the relation between the glassed and textile layers, and the cantilevered areas of the upper floor contribute to a varied spatial strategy providing a rich spatial experience.

Each of the house's four layers offers specific structural, material, functional, spatial and climatic qualities. The three envelopes perform on a number of levels where the polycarbonate shell and the fabric membrane are of special interest due to their performative qualities. Providing a protective sheath, the fabric membrane, consisting of a woven textile energy screen and insect membrane, employs different degrees of transparency resulting in varying views while still open to breezes during the summer. The question is whether such an approach can become increasingly locally specific by drawing more on the latent potential of non-standard architecture?

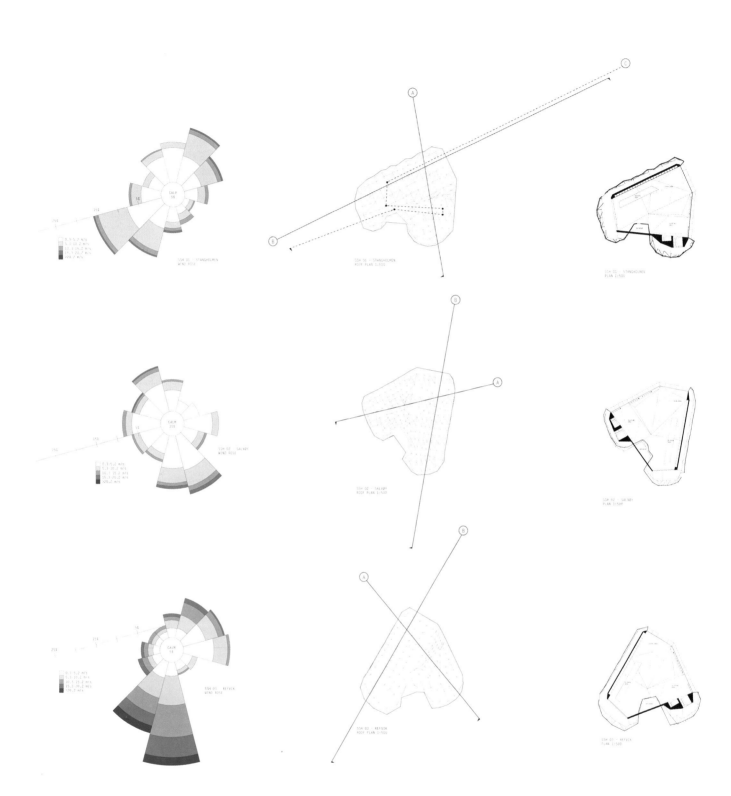

SSH 01 - STANGHOLMEN
WIND ROSE

SSH 01 - STANGHOLMEN
ROOF PLAN 1:500

SSH 01 - STANGHOLMEN
PLAN 1:500

SSH 02 - SALVØY
WIND ROSE

SSH 02 - SALVØY
ROOF PLAN 1:500

SSH 02 - SALVØY
PLAN 1:500

SSH 03 - REFVIK
WIND ROSE

SSH 03 - REFVIK
ROOF PLAN 1:500

SSH 03 - REFVIK
PLAN 1:500

Joakim Hoen,
Seaside
Second Home,
south and
west coast,
Norway,
2012-

Prevailing wind
directions, plans
and sections.

SSH 01 STANGHOLMEN
SECTION A 1:500

SSH 01 - STANGHOLMEN
SECTION B 1:500

SSH 02 SALVØY
SECTION A 1:500

SSH 02 - SALVØY
SECTION B 1:500

SSH 03 REFVIK
SECTION A 1:500

SSH 03 - REFVIK
SECTION B 1:500

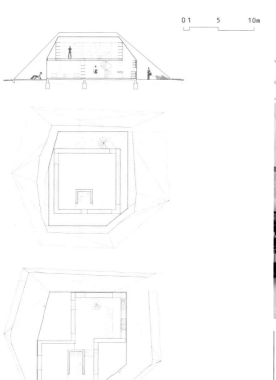

0 1   5   10m

top left: Section and plans of the Wall House.

top right (all): The Wall House is spatially organised by way of the layering of three envelopes that generate degrees of shelter and enclosure.

FAR frohn&rojas, Wall House, Santiago de Chile, 2007

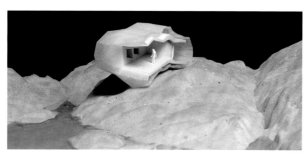

Joakim Hoen, Seaside Second Home, south and west coast, Norway, 2012–

Sectional rapid prototype model of version 01 of the Second Seaside Home.

above: Interior of version 01 of the Seaside Second Home.

below: Rendered views of version 02 of the Seaside Second Home in its context on the rocky seaside outcrops of the southwest Norwegian shoreline.

Locally Specific Data-Driven Design

The unbuilt Seaside Second Home project by Joakim Hoen pursues this potential through the development of custom-configured data-driven design methods and tools that are fed by locally specific data. Combining a series of spatial strategies with the non-standard approach, three individual buildings were designed for three particular sites. Situated in rocky terrain close to the ocean on the southwest coast of Norway, the sites share congruent and exposed conditions. Programmatically similar, the buildings relate to the specific terrain form as well as the climatic conditions and exposure of each site. The existing terrain was to be preserved and the specific terrain form of each location was derived from detailed laser scans to inform the architectural design. Data on local climate, such as site-specific wind conditions, as input into the generative design process was delivered by local weather stations, while solar impact was evaluated by means of computer-aided analysis.

Each of the three variants consisted of an interior open space articulated as an extension of the landscape and two layers that make up the building envelope: an inner climate envelope of variable thickness and an outer permeable screen sheltering a transitional zone. The interior space has a sectional articulation defined and constrained by considerations pertaining to providing or obstructing sightlines. Variable thickness of the inner, climatic envelope evolved from algorithmic procedures pertaining to its inner and outer surface and from nesting alcoves and shelves within the thickness of the envelope. The outer permeable envelope is a screen the articulation of which is generated by horizontal wind-loads, modulation of solar impact on the inner envelope and deceleration of airflow velocity from the exterior to the transitional space. The outer screen-like envelope and the outer surface of the inner envelope articulate the transitional space based on combined spatial requirements, needs for different activities and environmental performance.

A Combinatory Approach

The Seaside Second Home project clearly resonates with that of the Wall House by FAR frohn&rojas. Both deploy the non-standard approach to the design and materialisation of the architectures. Seaside Second Home takes the question of local specificity effectively further by addressing it in an integrated conceptual and methodological manner. Yet, while the production of a unified toolset may seem tempting, different modes and combinations of methods and tools are necessary to address combinations of local conditions that are not only different in degree, but also in kind. Prescriptive finite approaches run counter to the intent of deriving locally specific architectures. If the objective is to engender locally specific performative architecture and environment interactions, it would seem evident that no singular architectural expression or style could result from this, but rather a new attitude and approach to architectural design. ⌂

Notes
1. Frédéric Migayrou and Zeynep Mennan (eds), *Architectures Non Standard*, Éditions du Centre Pompidou (Paris), 2003
2. Branko Kolarevic, *Architecture in the Digital Age: Design and Manufacturing*, Taylor & Francis/Spon Press (London), 2003, p 42.
3. Kenneth Frampton, 'Towards a Critical Regionalism: Six Points for an Architecture of Resistance', in Hal Foster (ed), *The Anti-Aesthetic: Essays on Postmodern Culture*, Bay Press (Port Townsend, WA), 1983, p 21.
4. *Ibid*, p 17.
5. Kenneth Frampton, 'Ten Points on an Architecture of Regionalism: A Provisional Polemic' [1987], in Vincent B Canizaro (ed), *Architectural Regionalism: Collected Writings on Place, Identity, Modernity, and Tradition*, Princeton Architectural Press (New York), 2007, pp 375–85.

top: Solar impact analysis of the outer screen-like envelope.

centre: Unfolded (left) and principal (right) geometry of the outer screen-like envelope.

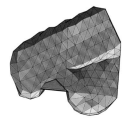

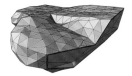

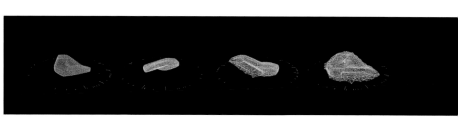

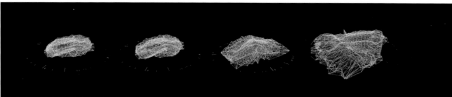

Data-driven generative design process, utilising airflow as the generator for the outer screen-like envelope.

The current speed of growth of the built environment is staggering and the existing global building stock immense. In this context one may wonder what to do with all the existing architectures that are ill equipped to provide reasonably habitable interior or exterior spaces for a broad range of uses. Clearly the swift replacement of entire architectures on a large scale is not feasible. Other options include extensive building adaptation or the implementation of compensatory technology, yet both are costly and often not sustainable. Today's preferred option is the technological modulation of interior and sometimes exterior climate conditions by way of heating, cooling, air-conditioning and so on. Yet, the question is whether architectures can do so without added mechanical-electrical equipment?

For the existing built environment there is another option: supplementing it with auxiliary architectures within, around and between existing architectures. These can be designed in close consideration of their interaction with the local physical environment. Needless to say, this approach is not new. There are, for instance, numerous historical examples of textile membranes as shading and sheltering devices, such as the sun sails used in the Mediterranean, the Spanish toldos, and corresponding systems in Japan and elsewhere that are used homogeneously to shade the street space between or adjacent to buildings.[1] If, however, a more differentiated modulation of light, ventilation and shelter is required, there are only a few examples at hand.

OCEAN Design Research Association and Izmir University of Economics, Luminous Veil, Izmir, Turkey, 2009

opposite bottom left: The textile screen wall enhances the light conditions in the dark space during the early evening hours.

Michael Hensel

Augmenting Existing Architectures with Performative Capacities

Auxiliary Architectures

Auxiliary architectures are a feature of many local building traditions across the world. Sited adjacent to existing structures, they are most often built as a means of tempering the climate, frequently offering additional shade in the summer months. Here Guest-Editor **Michael Hensel** proposes the development of auxiliary architectures as a solution to retrofitting and readapting existing building stock as climate conditions globally become increasingly unpredictable. He showcases the research that he has undertaken in the field in collaboration with the OCEAN Design Research Association, Scarcity and Creativity Studio (SCL) and Extended Threshold Studio.

Members of the OCEAN Design Research Association
have been designing and analysing differentiated
textile membrane systems since the early 2000s.[2]
This includes on the one hand the design and
implementation of such systems to establish production
and assembly procedures, while on the other obtaining
empirical data pertaining to the performance of the
systems and therefore the provisions afforded by them.
It includes the development of design methods that
utilise local data in the process of articulating textile
auxiliary architectures. These research-by-design efforts
take place predominantly in integrated research
and educational contexts such as the Advanced
Computational Design Laboratory and the Scarcity
and Creativity Studio at the Oslo School of
Architecture and Design.

The Luminous Veil project was designed and
implemented in 2009 by OCEAN with architecture
students at the Izmir University of Economics in Turkey.
Here the membrane system is implemented on a scale
and range of provisions akin to screen walls. The use
of a form-found tension-active membrane system in
conjunction with a cable net spatially articulates the
screen with the array of geometrically individually
articulated and rotated textile membranes constituting
a deep structure. The Luminous Veil is installed in a
corridor that needs shading and glare protection during
the early hours of the day while at the same time not
resulting in a dark space, and illumination during the
later hours of the day. This design experiment illustrates
how an auxiliary architecture can be implemented within
an existing building.

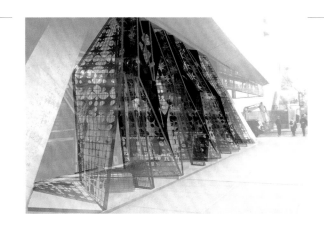

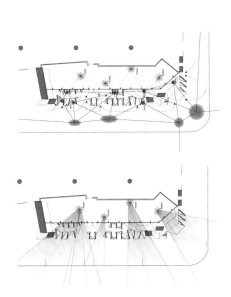

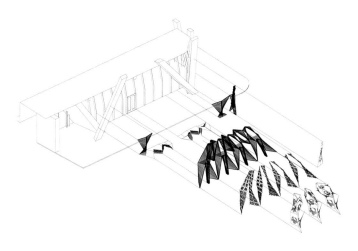

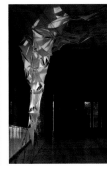

In a similar manner, OCEAN's unbuilt scheme for the M-Velope project in New York, designed in 2008, consists of an exterior textile and steel-mesh screen wall. Designed for an adjacent gallery, the membrane screen together with the glassed climate envelope result in a semi-sheltered transitional or interstitial space. The membrane screen wall provides nuanced modulation of views, light, shading, glare control, solar heat gains and ventilation. The combination of steel frame, mesh and textile elements makes it possible to change and adapt the membrane screen according to requirements pertaining to exhibitions in the gallery and seasonal climate change and related changes in the pattern of use of the street space.

Auxiliary architectures need not always be applied to already existing architectures; they can also be co-developed alongside new architectural design to expand the range of associated provisions. Examples include projects designed and built by the Scarcity and Creativity Studio (see pp 48–57) such as the Las Piedras del Cielo (2012) in the Open City in Ritoque, and the Community Centre in Pumanque (2014), both in Chile. Alternatively, auxiliary architectures may be designed without associated architecture as an individual provision, such as OCEAN's Membrella Canopy (2008).

The development of designs such as these benefits from physical form-finding experiments as well as data-driven computational processes. Directed by OCEAN members, the Extended Threshold Studio and the Advanced Computational Design Studio at the Oslo School of Architecture, for example, focus on the design of auxiliary architecture for neglected urban public spaces and developing design methods

Scarcity and Creativity Studio (SCL), Las Piedras del Cielo, Open City, Ritoque, Chile, 2012

top left: Analysis of the impact of the frequently severe Pacific coastal winds that cause on average more damage at the coast in Chile than earthquakes.

bottom: The project in the context of the Pacific coastal dune landscape of the Open City.

OCEAN Design Research Association, Membrella Canopy deployable prototype, 2008

top right (both): Visualisation of light modulation and shading pattern.

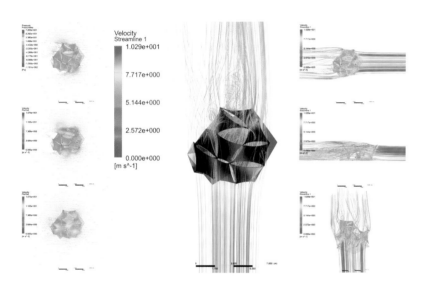

top: Analysis of light conditions on the membrane and the ground.

Extended Threshold Studio, Vika Membrane Canopy, Oslo, 2012

centre left: Rendering of the complex membrane canopy for a neglected urban public space, providing shelter for various outdoor activities during all seasons.

centre right: Augmented reality visualisation of the membrane canopy and time-specific shading pattern.

bottom: Elevation of the membrane canopy.

and tools for this purpose. This frequently involves integrating physical form-finding methods and computational associative modelling with local weather data input based on custom-made weather stations, and the deployment of artificial and virtual reality (AR/VR) visualisation tools to make the interaction between architectures and environment tangible for architects.

Research-by-design work in the studios concentrates on utilising different kinds of data to facilitate iterations between design and analysis. This includes the collection of locally specific weather data by way of the custom-made weather stations that directly feed data into computational models. This approach takes care of local climate variations and peak conditions that occur in specific sites that are not usually addressed by off-the-shelf software

packages that operate on averages. Locally specific real-time data sets are thus deployed to facilitate a much more nuanced understanding of the conditions that precede the design to enable detailed analysis prior to implementation, as well as post-occupation analysis in which the use of sensor networks, not unlike the network of weather stations, is becoming more common.[3]

The types of work discussed above extend the scope and inquiry from concept and design development and analysis to questions of workflow, workspace, tools and techniques, and the way architectural practice will need to be rethought in order to acquire the capacity for cutting-edge, performance-oriented design for the new and potentially vast market segment of auxiliary architectures.[4] ᗡ

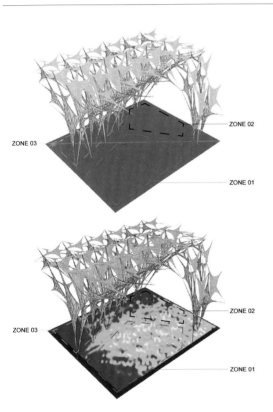

ZONE 03
ZONE 02
ZONE 01

ZONE 03
ZONE 02
ZONE 01

Notes
1. See for instance Georgina Krause-Valdinos (ed), *Schattenzelte: Sun and Shade – Toldos, Vela*, IL Vol 30, Institute for Lightweight Structures (Stuttgart), 1984.
2. See for instance Michael U Hensel and Achim Menges, 'Membrane Spaces', in Michael U Hensel and Achim Menges (eds), ᗡ *Versatility and Vicissitude: Performance in Morpho-Ecological Design*, March/April (no 2), 2008, pp 74–9, and Michael U Hensel and Defne Sunguroğlu Hensel, 'Extended Thresholds III: Auxiliary Architectures', in Hülya Ertaş, Michael U Hensel and Defne Sunguroğlu Hensel (eds), ᗡ *Turkey: At the Threshold*, January/February (no 1), 2010, pp 76–83.
3. In industrial agriculture the use of sensor networks is today quite common and architects can learn a lot from the way they are deployed in this context, in particular when architectures are intended to underpin ecology and biodiversity conservation efforts.
4. The topic of auxiliary architectures and some of the projects introduced above are discussed in greater detail in Michael U Hensel's ᗡ Primer *Performance-Oriented Architecture: Rethinking Architectural Design and the Built Environment*, John Wiley & Sons Ltd (Chichester), 2013.

The term 'nesting' corresponds to the structural and spatial principle used for developing an unreinforced masonry shell made up of a single layer of bricks, laid on face. It also refers to a specific process of designing with arches and vaults that gives rise to 'spheriodality', meaning curvilinear form or curved space, and possible structural hierarchy. The latter expands the set of conditions within which space can be formed across scale levels according to usage and in relation to changes in the environment. The Nested Catenaries design and construction system research project at the Oslo School of Architecture and Design (AHO) is based on this principle and process of nesting.[1] The advancement of structural masonry in architecture and engineering follows a long lineage with the true arch traced back to 4000 BC Mesopotamia. This cultural development can be mapped according to the design capabilities concerning functional integration and adaptability of properties to local environment and ecology. The ongoing Nested Catenaries research is built upon this historical background, and those examples that have contributed to the potentials of masonry shells in architecture, applied to local specificity.

Developmental Role of Structural Hierarchy

The Nested Catenaries system displays structural and spatial organisation across several length scales. This results in multifunctional and adaptive properties relative to scale and environment, and makes it possible to use locally specific conditions as design drivers. Hierarchical structure has been a topic of interest both in natural and cultural studies. Roderic Lakes discussed this concept not only in descriptive terms based on the recognition that 'structural features occur on different size scales', but also regarding the role of structural hierarchy in determining useful physical properties, suggesting the potential applicability of this idea to the analysis and design of materials and structures.[2] In support of this view, he compared the third-order hierarchical framework of the Eiffel Tower (the struts are organised across three size scales) with the single-order Centre Pompidou, which highlighted the structural and material advantages of the former, and gave examples from hierarchical cellular solids such as rocks, wood and bone, considered as solid and air/space composite.

So far seven levels of structural hierarchy have been considered: material at the micro scale; masonry material (brick, dried at low temperatures rather than high, and mortar); a single arch; a single vault; first-level nesting of three vaults; three-dimensional spatial extension based on sinusoidal directrix; and expansion with second-level nesting of 12 vaults. Structural hierarchy has several advantages: improved hyperstatism or topological toughening[3] – a response to the static indeterminacy of masonry structures that provides safety in case of local failure, for instance by way of multiple load paths for improved distribution of loads that allow effective use of material properties; reduced dependency on formwork and ease of construction; and as a key source for functional integration and adaptivity. Function entails the process of carrying out work (supporting loads, keeping warm, capturing sunlight) that arises out of the interaction between architecture and environment. Properties such as stiffness, curvature, porosity, self-shading, self-similarity, symmetry and asymmetry can in this context be informed by, and formed as a reaction to, local circumstances and conditions.

Structural hierarchy underlies developmental plasticity, which implies more than one path to a design solution. This is key for moving from general Nested Catenaries properties towards one that can be informed by specific requirements and local conditions, and foregrounds properties of flexibility in proportioning: structural independence from

A Developmental Route to Local Specificity

Nested Catenaries

Architect **Defne Sunguroğlu Hensel** and engineer **Guillem Baraut Bover** describe the Nested Catenaries design and construction system they have developed as part of a research project at the Oslo School of Architecture and Design (AHO). They explain how their innovative development of an unreinforced masonry shell structure made up of a single layer of bricks is informed by ancient building traditions and has been further evolved to be attuned to local context.

**Defne Sunguroğlu Hensel
and Guillem Baraut Bover**

Defne Sunguroğlu Hensel,
Nested Catenaries
condition-effect-property
chart,
2014

Chart mapping the conditions
(including material/structure and
environment), effects/events and
properties registered across several
scales of magnitude.

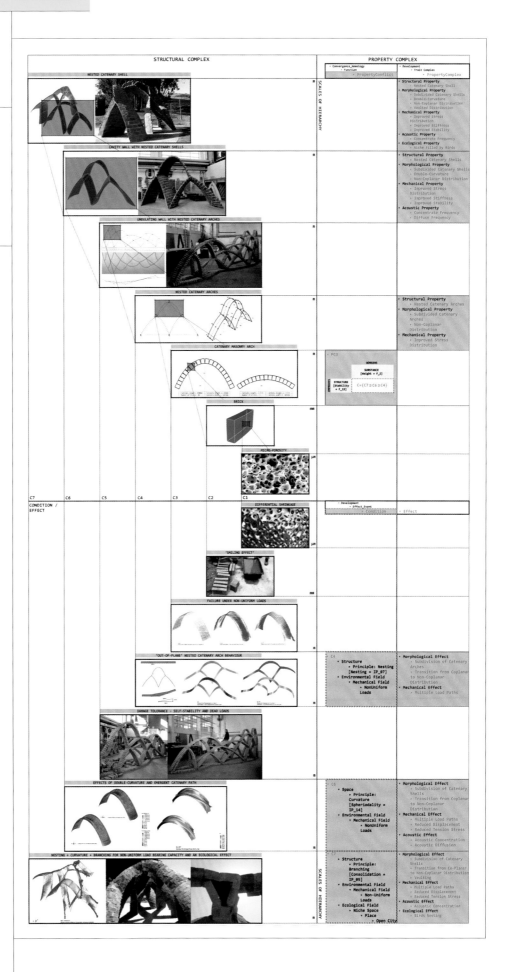

Defne Sunguroğlu Hensel, Guillem Baraut Bover and Øyvind Buset, Nested Catenaries cavity wall, Oslo School of Architecture and Design (AHO) construction hall, Oslo, 2012

top left: The design involved the use of three shells, two of which could be articulated independently while remaining in relation to the third shell above. These are catenary shells with synclastic and anticlastic surface curvatures connected with the shell above, which displays a transition from a concave to convex transverse section. The reason for two different base-shell solutions was to study their implications for construction and structural behaviour under non-uniform loads.

symmetry, freedom from uniform repetition, and geometric unconstraint from compression-only forms. This entails a shift from a generalised prototype to a system that can be specific to the conditions of each setting in which it is to be implemented in an architectural design; in other words, from a general condition–effect–property chart to a project-specific one.

Functional Integration and Local Adaptivity

To date, the Nested Catenaries system has been taken through three stages of development, in the form of an undulating arched wall[4] and cavity wall[5] that were built in the AHO construction hall, and a Nested Catenaries shell located in Chile[6] that is subjected to high seismic impact. The focus thus far has been on the structural and spatial potentials in this architectural approach to the catenary problem to demonstrate the advantages of nesting, curvature and branching for creating structural properties that are useful for load-bearing functions, while offering a high stiffness-to-weight ratio for multiple load cases.

The Nested Catenaries shell in Chile has withstood several earthquakes of magnitudes up to seven on the Richter scale. The next phase will focus on further developing the material, structural and spatial potentials by expanding the environmental, ecological and social factors considered and the way the system can be articulated in relation to locally specific circumstances.

Masonry is statically indeterminate: from unpredictable initial small displacements can arise large deviations from the actual thrust line.[7] Multiple load-cases therefore need to consider the safety factor. If emergent thrust lines within material thickness are not sustained, tension concentrations may be generated, leading to fracture and eventual failure as a consequence of the low tensile strength of the masonry. Stability with an emphasis on shape independent of scale, strength of material and foundation, and adherence to the rules of proportion and symmetry have thus been considered in general as primary parameters for any structural masonry. Typically, the common response to constraints associated with masonry are: reduction of unpredictability to a minimum by eliminating the impact of environmental, ecological influences; functional decomposition – a one-to-

Defne Sunguroğlu Hensel, Guillem Baraut Bover and Øyvind Buset, Nested Catenaries shell, Open City, Ritoque, Chile, 2012

left: This project was built as an extension to the cemetery at the Open City. The design constitutes 12 sub-shells of varying size, creating a volume of 162 cubic metres (5,721 cubic feet), each with synclastic surface geometry to retain the complexity of construction, according to the allocated time.

top right and right: The digital model of the formwork on site and selected instances from the iterative stages of topological optimisation that improve load distribution and reduce critical stress concentrations to admissible range.

Defne Sunguroğlu Hensel
and Øyvind Buset,
Nested Catenaries
undulating arched
wall, workshop with the
Auxiliary Architectures
Studio, Oslo School of
Architecture and Design
(AHO), Oslo,
2010

Analogue and computer-generated
15 interacting catenary geometry
for an undulating wall, using
the hanging model and Rhino
Kangaroo physics engine.

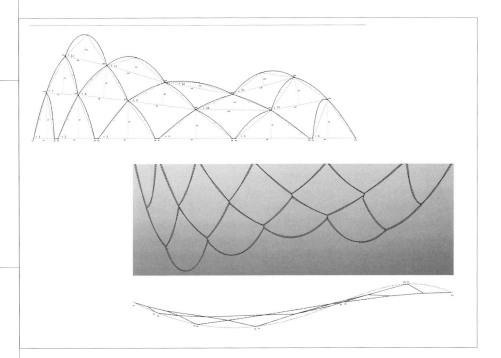

The final self-standing structure. A symmetrical
wall was built initially to provide mutual support
and compensate for the lack of necessary structural
calculations at the time. Upon removal of the
formworks, used in the overall construction of 30
arches, the support was proved to be unnecessary and
was therefore removed. Its three-dimensional spatial
organisation is contrasted with the smaller structure,
on the right, showing a linear arrangement.

one mapping between structural and functional modules as
opposed to integration; or increasing thickness, reinforcement
or combining materials.

Structural independence from mass by way of reducing
thickness and weight while maintaining stability and stiffness
(displacement of mass with space) remains a key driver in the
evolutionary development of masonry.[8] However, mass is not
only a vital structural attribute; it is also essential for thermal
behaviour and for the embedding of spaces of various sizes
(cavities, recesses, alcoves or niches) within the thickness of
the wall or vault.

Introducing openings without compromising structure
is a major benefit, but which properties are affected when
mass is reduced, and what are the consequences for spatial
organisation? This question indicates the need for functional
integration. Property conflicts arise either from incompatible
requirements or not well-understood interrelations between
variables, which often results in improving one parameter
while compromising another. This implies that the adaptive
capacity of masonry systems needs to be better integrated
with local conditions.

In the context of a Master's-level workshop at AHO,
work focused on Eladio Dieste's Gaussian and freestanding
vaults, and the possibility of liberating these from symmetry
and uniform axial repetition.[9] This was accomplished
through computational associative modelling. The breaking
of symmetry enables an improved orientation of portions
of the building volume and the geometrically varied vaults
to environmental conditions such as sun path and angle,
and prevailing wind directions, as well as the adaptation of
the design to irregular terrain and building plots. Dieste's
Church of Christ the Worker (1960) in Atlántida, Uruguay,
for instance, consists of vaults and longitudinal perimeter
walls that form continuous sinusoidal surfaces. Each vault
segment displays a two-axial symmetry and a mono-axial
directionality, and both properties limit the possibility of
proportioning and orienting the building and its parts in
a differentiated way. The associative model that was built
during the course of the workshop enabled release from these
constraints, but at the same time needed to comply with the
limitations of the structural system and the inherent relation
between form and structure, in order to expand to a varied
form, structure and environment relation.

A remarkable example that makes exceptional use of
masonry for combined environmental and social functions,
but independent of structure, are Islamic screen walls, such
as the mashrabiya (made from wood), or the Mogul jali
(made of stone). Hassan Fathy elaborated the characteristics
of these screen walls by considering the material-specific
parameters, the size, shape and distribution of interstices and
balusters, and the screen pattern and its spatial organisation
in relation to the integrated functions of thermal, light
(glare), airflow, moisture and view control and regulation.[10]

Eladio Dieste, Church
of Christ the Worker,
Atlántida, Uruguay,
1960

opposite right: An external view of
the building showing the undulating
wall and roof with particular attention
to their combined effect.

right: The digital associative models
and shading analysis of some of
the geometric variants of Dieste's
Church of Christ the Worker.

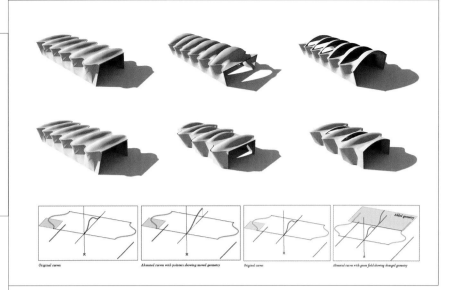

Computing Dieste's vaults, workshop
with the Auxiliary Architectures
Studio, Oslo School of Architecture
and Design (AHO), Oslo,
2010

right and below: Some of the results from the
workshop showing the computational associative
models of Dieste's Port Warehouse, Montevideo,
Uruguay, 1979.

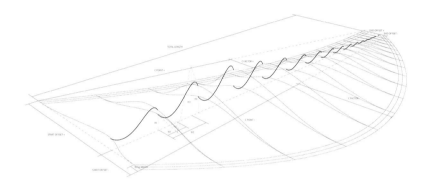

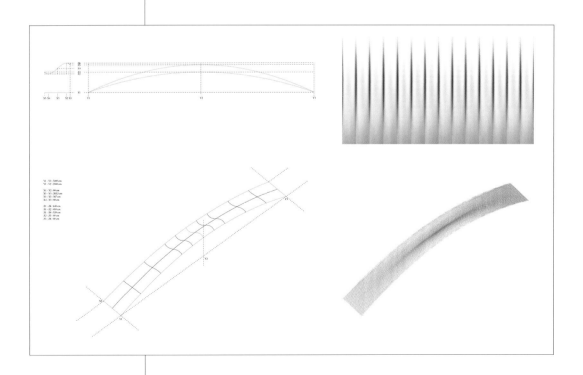

Arriving at such a level of extended functional integration, including structural capacity, is the ambition for the next stage in the development of the Nested Catenaries system.

New Paths

A critical factor for any masonry structure is the treatment of the foundation and ground datum. In the next stage of the Nested Catenaries development, the intention is to move away from reinforced-concrete slab foundations towards a solution developed according to spheriodality or the three-dimensional spatial concept of the vault, with a reduced environmental-ecological footprint and an improved locally specific response to the ground. This approach is based on a two-way feedback between the ground and the Nested Catenaries system, which expands on the form-finding process, informed by both the physical properties of the ground and the reaction forces that translate the former into a topographical map. This can be considered either as tension-driven carving or a process of local strengthening, maintaining or adding material wherever necessary and useful, and in so doing creating a particular terrain form.

Difficulties in analysing and understanding masonry behaviour have largely limited the vault to uniform repetition, symmetrical arrangements as can been seen, for instance, in cathedrals, and axial-field arrays such as hypostyle halls like that of the Great Mosque of Cordoba. Due to this homogeneous treatment, the irregularities of sites have been seen as disadvantages. Instead of being integrated in both the design process and the resulting architectures, they have been eliminated to create a homogeneous ground.

The slenderness of Nested Catenaries vaults can reduce impact on the ground to a necessary minimum. The design of the first Nested Catenaries shell focused on a particular three-dimensional spatial organisation of smaller interconnected sub-shells that are nested into two cavity walls. This produced features that evoke chambers, cavities, recesses, alcoves or niches as spatial potentials for differentiation, organised along the perimeter of larger spaces that arise from the overall arrangement of the system. These can include centric, polycentric, single- or poly-directional arrangements or interstitial spaces between independent or interdependent parts of a Nested Catenaries system. This approach departs from the more typical spatial model of arches and vaults organised along a central axis with adjoining secondary vaults to form arcades or chambers in the perimeter, as seen in churches or cathedrals. Instead the intent is orientational flexibility that can facilitate the material and spatial organisation to be informed by local irregularities of the site and according to the particularities of environmental conditions and use requirements and intentions. In instances where the overall shell distribution is limited, other variables including shell depth and transverse curvature can be activated, made possible by the multi-level hierarchical structure of the system.

Formation and multiplication of ground, not only in terms of soil depth but also height, requires expansion of the vault's structural capacity to include live loads. The principle of merging, which implies transforming a single shell into a fractal-like composition, can improve structural support due to increased redundancy via added structural hierarchy, but also offer environmental benefits when designing spaces for different climatic needs and conditions.

Changes in density, distribution and scale of arches or vaults that increases surface area can serve to improve both structural and environmental behaviour. This can be further improved by the degree and type of enclosure, as well as at the micro scale by utilising the porosity of bricks for thermal resistance. The latter is a direct product of brick's microstructure, porosity, density, moisture content and absolute temperature, as well as its thickness. Interestingly, if changes in thickness were the only variable, this would lead to an opposing relation of structural and environmental behaviour, but if we tend towards a denser, merged, sponge-like materiality the structure will remain low-weight while acting as a thermal insulator. When considering resistance to heat, synclastic surface curvature is a better option for providing shade than an anticlastic shell, although surface orientation is one possibility for improvement.

Exposed surface curvature is a much-used feature in traditional Islamic architectures with a multitude of domes adorning roof surfaces. Curvature provides self-shading of parts of the exposed surface at almost all times of the day. The heated surface area is cooled through the absorption of heat by the cooler areas, thus improving thermal resistance. It is also possible that the same operates in reverse in more moderate climates to maximise heat gain during the cold seasons. Critical design parameters include the level of porosity across scales, as well as depth, height, width and orientation of the shell curvature. Likewise, porosity on the scale of the shells can imply creating a screen wall not unlike the Brazilian Cobogó (often seen as concrete facade features used for environmental regulation, coined by three Brazilian engineers in the early 20th century) or a Mogul jali.

In the further development of the Nested Catenaries system, emphasis is being placed on principles, models and processes that inform the design in relation to usage and specific local settings by utilising all levels of system hierarchy. In so doing, what once began as a generalised prototype becomes individually varied specific design instances that are particularised at many system scales and spatial organisations, arriving at an integral relation not only of form, material and structure, but also of space and local environment. ∆

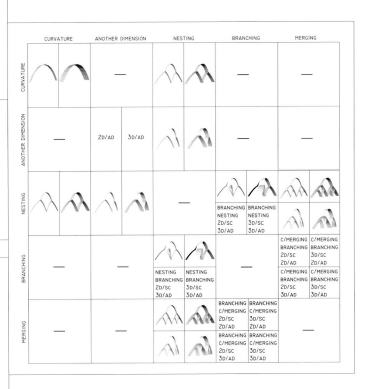

Defne Sunguroğlu Hensel, Nested Catenaries principles matrix, 2014

The matrix shows the different principles underlying the Nested Catenaries design system. One is 'Merging', which is highlighted in red. This principle will be explored as a structural and environmental strategy.

Defne Sunguroğlu Hensel, Guillem Baraut Bover and Øyvind Buset, Nested Catenaries shell, Open City, Ritoque, Chile, 2012

The finite element method can be used in the generation of terrain form with load-bearing capacity: (a) top view of the Nested Catenaries shell built in Chile and its foundation slab; (b) the main axial forces in the ground slab formed during peak seismic loads in the X-direction; (c) the values simulated with contour lines, representing specific axial forces. Due to the linear relation between the axial tension force and the foundation thickness, this contour map can be directly translated into a new ground form.

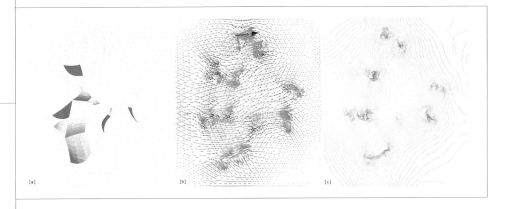

[a]   [b]   [c]

Notes

1. The Nested Catenaries research is part of the Defne Sunguroğlu Hensel's doctoral studies and has been carried out through a close collaboration with Guillem Baraut Bover (engineer) and Øyvind Buset (master mason). See Defne Sunguroğlu Hensel and Guillem Baraut Bover, 'Nested Catenaries', *Journal of the International Association for Shell and Spatial Structures,* 1, 54, 2013, pp 39–55.
2. Roderic Lakes, 'Materials with Structural Hierarchy', *Nature,* 361, 1993, pp 511–15.
3. Michael F Ashby, 'Hybrids to Fill Holes in Material Property Space', *Philosophical Magazine,* 85, 26, 2005, pp 3235–57.
4. Master's-level workshop with the Auxiliary Architectures Studio, Oslo School of Architecture and Design (AHO), Nested Catenaries, Phase 1, Oslo, 2010. See: www.ocean–designresearch.net for the full credit list.
5. Auxiliary Architectures Studio, Nested Catenaries, Phase 2, AHO, Oslo, 2012. See: www.ocean–designresearch.net for the full credit list.
6. Auxiliary Architectures Studio, Open City workshop, Nested Catenaries, Phase 3, Open City, Ritoque, Chile,

2012. See: www.ocean–designresearch.net for the full credit list.
7. Jacques Heyman, *The Stone Skeleton: Structural Engineering of Masonry Architecture,* Cambridge University Press (Cambridge), 1995.
8. Some innovative solutions include: the multiple load paths as seen in Roman architecture and Gothic cathedrals; St Paul's Cathedral's (1675–1710) triple dome with the catenary applied to the middle layer; the Catalan vaults including the Vapor Aymerich textile factory (1908) and its further advancement by Guastavino,

such as the Batlló factory (1868–9); Gaudí's three-dimensional advancement of the hanging model (1898–1908) for the Colònia Güell Chapel (1914); and Dieste's freestanding and Gaussian vaults of Cerámica Armada.
9. Defne Sunguroğlu Hensel, Auxiliary Architectures studio workshop, AHO, Oslo, 2010.
10. Hassan Fathy, *Natural Energy and Vernacular Architecture: Principles and Examples with Reference to Hot and Arid Climates,* University of Chicago Press (Chicago, IL and London), 1986, p 46.

Areti Markopoulou and Rodrigo Rubio

Smart Living Architecture

—

Solar Prototypes

IAAC
Endesa Pavilion
Barcelona

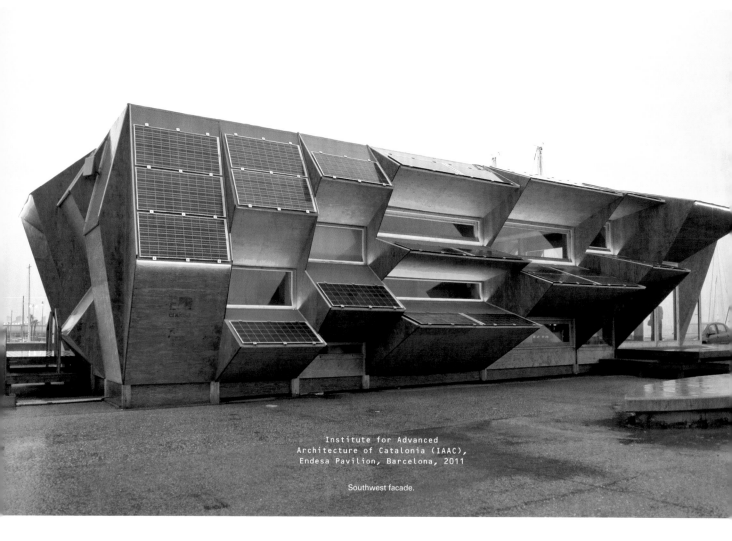

Institute for Advanced
Architecture of Catalonia (IAAC),
Endesa Pavilion, Barcelona, 2011

Southwest facade.

Areti Markopoulou and Rodrigo Rubio of the Institute for Advanced Architecture of Catalonia (IAAC) describe how the institute's Endesa Pavilion in Barcelona responds to the contemporary challenge of constructing intelligent and sustainable prototypes, as a structure that interacts and exchanges resources with its environment. Parametrically designed, it reacts to the data of its specific solar site, and via its flexible solar cells generates twice as much energy as it consumes.

As Information Era technologies and their impacts on architecture change, their relationship calls for new or adapted concepts, where buildings and cities seamlessly intertwine with digital content, and where the language of electronic connections ties in with that of physical connections. Architecture cannot be just inhabited and rigid; users and the environment should integrate with it. In the early 20th century, the concept of 'dwelling' was defined as a 'machine for living', a reference to a new way of understanding the construction of inhabitable spaces that characterised the Machine Age. A century later we face the challenge of constructing intelligent and sustainable prototypes, architectures that interact and interchange resources with their environment, following the principles of ecology or biology rather than those of mere construction.

Such architectures need to function as self-sufficient and responsive nodes with the capacity to use and produce resources. Additionally, the extended use of advanced materials enables architectures to adjust their properties to different environmental conditions, thus allowing the programming of buildings at a nanoscale and opening up a series of applications in the architecture of building skins and structures. The latter can operate in combination with artificial and computational intelligence, sensors and actuators, as well as advanced manufacturing techniques and bio-mimetic innovations to provide revolutionary ideas on growth, adaptability, repair, sensitivity, replication and energy savings in architecture.

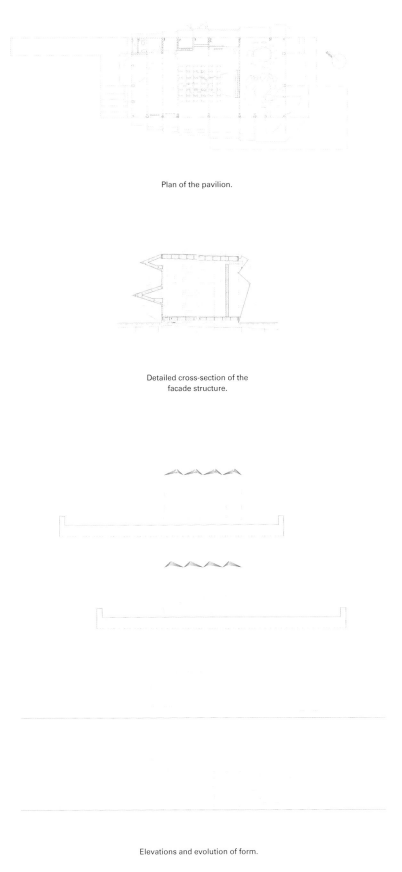

Plan of the pavilion.

Detailed cross-section of the facade structure.

Elevations and evolution of form.

Various stages of the construction process.

The Institute for Advanced Architecture of Catalonia (IAAC), an educational and research centre located in Barcelona, pursues an agenda focused on smart and self-sufficient buildings that includes the production of 1:1 scale constructions such as the Fab Lab House or the Endesa Pavilion, parametrically designed houses in which form follows the data of the solar path of their specific sites. Fab Lab House has been entirely digitally fabricated by a group of researchers and students, and is able to generate twice as much energy than it needs to consume via flexible solar cells that are adjusted to the optimum form of the building.

The Endesa Pavilion is a self-sufficient solar prototype installed at the Barcelona Olympic port within the framework of the Barcelona Smart City Expo World Congress 2011. Over a period of one year the project was used as a control room for the monitoring and testing of several projects related to intelligent power management. It is the first 1:1 prototype of a wooden solar-tracking facade system applicable to different scales and latitudes. The adaptive modular system is based on parametric modelling and digital fabrication, with an algorithm coded to optimise geometries depending on local conditions to create a constructive system that aims to integrate passive strategies with active ones, traditional knowledge with cutting-edge technology, and local conditions with global logics. The Endesa Pavilion is a skin that reads and renders legible the surrounding energetic conditions. It takes its energy from the sun, and its geometry from seasonal sun paths, shifting from the famous 20th-century mantra 'form follows function' to the 21st-century 'form follows energy'.

As a prototype, the pavilion researches the possibilities of combining traditional industry with contemporary digital fabrication techniques. Each facade module is calculated and generated using parametric design tools, fabricated by way of CNC milling micro-laminated wood panels, preassembled, transported and plugged into the structure. Conventional mass-production processes and new technologies, adapted to mass-customisation requirements, are interweaved in a single continuous workflow.

The pavilion is not a closed product, but a construction system. It is not intended as a definitive and finished icon, but rather as an open and multiscalar proposal. It is a facade system based on a set of mathematical rules and logics ready for export

Interior view of the pavilion during the Barcelona Smart City Expo World Congress in 2011.

and adaptable to different locations or materials in response to local conditions and available technologies and materials. Based on adaptation and not on repetition, it is able to read context conditions and respond to them. The Endesa Pavilion is therefore Barcelona's version of an adaptive code able to be applied (grafted) in different situations with different demands.

A simple logic drives the whole design. The relative position of each facade component with the different seasonal sun paths defines its geometry (openness, deepness and panelling inclinations). Each component is defined globally yet resolved locally, and calculated individually, module by module, following the same shared rules. Each generates its own energy, controls its own sun radiation, natural light and artificial interior and exterior illumination, storage, insulation, and so on, and contains and resolves locally numerous architectural requirements following a single shared logic. As each module is different because it is responding to slightly different conditions, the pavilion obtains a level of organic responsiveness that was unthinkable within traditional modelling systems and conventional means of fabrication.

The pavilion is now a totally self-sufficient building working exclusively with sun energy. However, smart cities are not made just out of smart buildings. It generates 140 per cent of the energy it consumes. The surplus of energy production could feed the consumption of one conventional household. The prototype at the Olympic port was used to perform experimental research on the digital management of energy grids by enabling digital control of energy flows, crossing real-time data with decision-making. The Internet of Energy[1] brings the flexibility of a Cloud to the physical world. Networking, collaborating and interchanging are essential means to make a cohesive resilient system. Hence new informational technologies, with their inherent open participatory character, are crucial tools.

Northwest and southwest facades.

Advances in building design and construction, however, cannot leave the urban scale unaffected. The Endesa prototype is a building strategy with urban effects. And this happens because each action on the territory implies a manipulation of multiple environmental forces, connected to numerous informational flows and networks such as energy, transport, logistics and information, generating new inhabitable and responsive nodes with the potential to use and produce resources. Territorial and urban strategies and building operations must therefore be coordinated processes that extend architectural knowledge to new forms of management and planning, in which multiscalar thinking also entails an understanding of shifting dynamics, energy and information transmission and continuous adaptation. ∆

Note
1. Ovidiu Vermesan/ SINTEF, 'Internet of Energy', Scandic Marina Congress Center, Helsinki, 26 October 2011: http://www.cleen. fi/fi/Markkinointiviestint/ Liite%207.%20Internet%20 of%20Energy_Ovidiu%20 Vermesan,SINTEF.pdf.

Southeast and southwest facades.

Antoni Gaudí,
Sagrada Família School,
Barcelona,
1909

The school is a prime example of an experimental and innovative architecture that had to operate on tightly limited resources.

Michael Hensel and Christian Hermansen Cordua

Outlook

En Route to Intensely Local Architectures and Tectonics

Guest-Editors **Michael Hensel and Christian Hermansen Cordua** reflect on four interrelated traits of current experimental practice that highlight the local: small size, locality, tectonics and experimentation/research. The objective is to provide an opening for further developments of the various trajectories of work that are featured in this issue, as well as for dedicated research. From this the contours of new 'schools of thought' can be seen to emerge, which render the notion of local architectures inherently pluralistic, thus transcending the perception that this type of work has to be bound by singular regional styles, types or identities.

OCEAN Design Research Association,
Arrayed Membrane Canopy Research,
2008-

The development of design systems, rather than universal
prototypes, facilitates the particularisation of each design
for each setting in relation to the required associated
performative capacities, such as spatial articulation and
environmental modulation.

OCEAN Design Research Association, Bylgia
Membrane Array, FRAC Centre, Orléans,
France,
2008

Experimental construction of full-scale location-specific
arrayed membrane systems studies and develops the design
system in terms of its performative capacities and process and
detailing of construction.

OCEAN Design
Research
Association and
Izmir University
of Economy,
Luminous Veil,
Izmir, Turkey,
2009

Climate change, environmental threats,[1] the ongoing repercussions of the 2008 financial crash, and the exclusion of the interest of communities from the planning process[2] appear to have a considerable impact on architectural sensibilities. It seems that the 1990s and 2000s 'everything goes' attitude of highly styled idiosyncratic architectures has come to a close and that nondescript commercial architectures produced by global corporate firms are now increasingly critically scrutinised. This is not to say that such trends do not continue wherever turbo capitalism still rules. However, there are new directions springing up in architecture that address questions above and beyond exclusively formal fixation, that emphasise more complex topics such as participation, resilience, scarcity, ecology and so on. The Dutch architect and educator Wiel Arets stated: 'If the boom years were about "starchitects" … the current era is both more practical and more collectivist'.[3] The aim of this issue of D has been to contribute to the definition of one of the new sensibilities by bringing together work that shares certain characteristics addressing the relation between global and local conditions, and developments in this field, through an experimental approach that plays out in modestly resourced small-scale projects. The traits that unite these works can be distilled into four concepts: small size, locality, tectonics, and experimentation/research.

Small Size

Recognising that large-scale projects frequently come at the expense of local cultures and environments, the work presented in this issue is almost invariably small in size. This is neither accidental nor the result of designers' inability to obtain larger commissions. Bigger offices often accept small-scale projects as a way of gaining experimental opportunities that can enrich the work of the practice at large, for instance designing pavilions for expos or special events and occasions, such as the Serpentine Gallery pavilions. Small buildings can sidestep some of the conditions that seem to be inherent in large projects: their ostensibly inescapable focus on economic gain, efficiency and also, increasingly, branding. In so doing small projects can offer more opportunities for experimentation and research, and encourage greater risk-taking.

Over the last two decades, many schools of architecture have instituted programmes that focus on the design and construction of pavilions and similar small-scale architectures. These include the School of Architecture and Design at the Pontifical Catholic University of Valparaíso in conjunction with the Open City in Ritoque, Chile (see pp 34–9), and Rural Studio at Auburn University in Alabama (pp 40–47)). While some of these efforts result in prototypical outcomes that are not per se locally specific, but could certainly become so, there is also a strand of work that aims for intensely local design, as the lines of works in this issue show. Similar tendencies are also apparent in practice, evidenced by the works of Studio Mumbai (pp 94–101), RCR Arquitectes, Rintala Eggertsson (pp 76–81) and many others. From this the question arises how the experiments and research findings may eventually inform medium- and larger-sized projects. While practice has its own particular constraints in addressing this, it is plausible that the impetus can come from schools of architecture and research organisations in collaboration with practice. Tightly knit relations between universities and small practices such as both Rintala Eggertsson and TYIN tegnestue with the Norwegian University of Science and Technology (NTNU) in Trondheim can be productive in enabling 'schools of thought' based on new types of partnership that spread risk and afford inroads into testing the findings at a larger scale.

Locality

What do we mean by 'local' in a context in which architects increasingly build globally? For us this question is located neither in a stylistic domain nor in some form of nostalgia for the past, but instead in deploying the potential of the resources of local cultures, and spatial and material organisations and practices, to project contemporary and forward-looking local architectures.

The work featured in this issue of D interprets 'local' in multiple ways. In the case of Rural Studio, local implies social commitment, and while their works are related to Alabama and, more specifically, to Hale County, their motives can well be seen to be of global relevance. Rintala and Eggertsson, on the other hand, depart from a global critique of our current condition, and the local emerges from their willingness to learn from the settings and histories they engage with in each specific project. Perhaps the case of the Open City shows most clearly that the conversation between the local and construction benefits from an ongoing process that escapes settling into a fixed stylistic canon and an identity that is arrested in time.

Scarcity and Creativity Studio (SCL),
Las Piedras del Cielo, Open City,
Ritoque, Chile,
2012

Scarcity and Creativity Studio (SCL),
Community Centre, Pumanque, Chile,
2014

The implementation of auxiliary arrayed membrane
systems in experimental design and built projects
analyses and instrumentalises the specific performance
capacities of the design system.

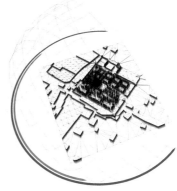

Sustainable Environment Association
(SEA), Performance capacity and
airflow analysis of the Fin Garden
and Kiosk (c 1629), Kashan, Iran,
2014

Analysis of the performance capacities of pre-industrial architectures frequently reveals interesting design potentials for contemporary strategies for intensely local architectures. The SEA currently undertakes a broad range of analyses of architectural case studies and settlement patterns that often involve the impact of context, such as the shading provided by adjacent vegetation.

Thus the door to contemporary versions of locally specific architectures has just opened. The contours of emerging 'schools of thought' about the local are beginning to take shape that may complement or offset more traditional understandings of regions defined by single boundaries in favour of local specificity defined by multiple boundaries addressing a range of interrelated developing themes. A further question then arises as to how heterogeneous cultures and societies, and those that undergo substantial changes, can be addressed? This is of immense political relevance today as diverse groupings and minorities increasingly demand greater independence and representation, a condition from which many conflicts are arising. As this relates to the evolution of identities over time, the impetus to arrest identities back into singular styles or approaches to local specificity in architectural design needs to be resisted. Contemporary approaches to the notion of the 'local' must be based on transformation over time and a productive pluralism.

Tectonics

The term 'tectonic' is applied here in Frampton's sense that architecture is as much about structure and construction as it is about spatial experience.[4] The works presented in this issue invariably reveal their tectonic qualities, the way they are structured and constructed, and how these two considerations are an integral part of the form and space of the building. Most of the small-scale projects featured require integration of objectives due to constrained means and resources, while at the same time the fact that the designers are often the builders entails that adjustments to designs can be made during construction and with the participation of locals. In some cases the intensive production of full-scale mock-ups, as in the work of Studio Mumbai or the early Renzo Piano Building Workshop (pp 88–101), advances the articulation and performative capacities of the tectonic solutions beyond that of everyday architectures. This usually concerns the performative capacities of architectures with regard to the relation between provisions for use, spatial organisation and environmental modulation, all of which constitute factors of local specificity and can be addressed in terms of tectonic articulation.

Experimentation/Research

Throughout architectural history, small buildings have been used as a means to search for and demonstrate in a clear way the potential of new directions for architecture. Built projects such as Antoni Gaudí's Sagrada Família School in Barcelona (1909), Richard Buckminster Fuller's Dymaxion House (1930, redesigned 1945) and Jean Prouvé's House for the Tropics (1949) come to mind as experimental buildings that signalled new directions for architecture. Likewise, pavilions, follies, exhibition architectures and other such projects highlight the potential of experimentation in terms of projecting architectural possibilities. This can be raised to a further level through research agendas that inform developments with longer time spans in which more general prototypes can be seen as principal design systems that result in locally specific iterations: the Nested Catenaries system by Defne Sunguroğlu Hensel and Guillem Baraut Bover (pp 120–27), or the Endesa Pavilion by the Institute for Advanced Architecture of Catalonia (IAAC) (pp 128–31), for example.

Designing Forward

Immediate considerations that focus on making provisions relevant to local circumstances, as well as the long-term enabling of change that avoids relentless replication of styles, types, identities or lifestyles and always thinks anew, may once again be central to architecture. How the above four themes and their inherent challenges are addressed will thus be a key determinant of the combined specificity, resilience and capacities of future architectures. ⌀

Notes

1. For instance, the 2012 Hurricane Sandy, the largest Atlantic hurricane on record with total damage surpassed only by Hurricane Katrina, became the catalyst for discussions about resilience.
2. See, for instance, the Gezi Park protests in Istanbul in 2013.
3. Robert Sharoff, 'A New Dean Promises to Shake Up IIT's Architecture School', *Crain's Chicago Business*, 9 October

2012: www.chicagobusiness.com/article/20121009/NEWS07/121009804/a-new-dean-promises-to-shake-up-iits-architecture-school.
4. See Kenneth Frampton in his *Studies in Tectonic Culture: The Poetics of Construction in Nineteenth and Twentieth Century Architecture*, MIT Press (Cambridge, MA), 1995.

By implication, the development of experimental architecture that is responsive to the local context can have sustainable benefits for the natural environment and adjacent community. Here, architect and writer **Terri Peters**, who has a PhD in sustainable building transformation, picks up the gauntlet and asks how the notion of localness might be able to advance sustainable design. Focusing on a qualitative rather than quantitative interpretation of sustainability, she describes projects by New York-based studio The Living, the Chinese architect Li Xiaodong and Toronto architects Superkül, highlighting the importance of ecology, social sustainability and context-specific design in the treatment of their work.

Architects learn by putting things together: constructing arguments, building prototypes, adding layers of meaning, material and culture to a place. This ⌀ provides a provocative discussion of the role of experimental constructions in architecture by connecting to the highly relevant concept of localness. Architecture is always in some way locally responsive, but here guest-editors Michael Hensel and Christian Hermansen Cordua examine a certain kind of context-specific architecture that is both about and of the local. As a response to globalisation, to the unchecked capitalism that makes global cities so similar, the issue reveals a broad range of approaches to experimentation, sometimes connecting the construction of these structures beyond themselves, in ways that might influence mainstream practice. It does not, however, explicitly pursue how localness can further sustainable design. Here it misses an opportunity to highlight ways the local can provide the seeds for a compelling and alternative approach to sustainable design.

Intensely local approaches to sustainable design can benefit architecture in all stages of the design process. For example, considering the broader ecology of the building process, using local materials can reduce the embodied energy in materials and component manufacture and transport. Relating to social sustainability, using local labour and expertise or providing local training opportunities adds a social and economic benefit to the larger community. Context- and climate-specific approaches

Sustaining the Local

Terri Peters

An Alternative Approach to Sustainable Design

COUNTERPOINT
02/2015
№ 234
⌀

The Living

Hy-Fi

MoMA PS1

New York

2014

left: Hy-Fi was a temporary summer pavilion installed in the MoMA PS1 courtyard as part of the Young Architects Program. The architectural experience was heightened by the choice of material. The small modules are stacked to form a complex roof space, while at ground level visitors experienced filtered daylight and a distinctive smell in the sculptural interior.

above: Hy-Fi compostable bricks. The organic tower was designed to be planted, to grow and die, composed of biodegradable, compostable modules formed from farm waste, mushroom roots and corn stalks grown in steel brick moulds. Researchers at Ecovative developed the material in 2007 and typically use it for packaging.

could include integrating with the existing architectural surroundings, and developing a place-based approach to the specific site. The concept of 'localness' has the power to bridge current discussions about sustainability in architecture, and potentially offers new ways of talking about and thinking about inherently non-architectural concepts. Sustainability is currently largely measured and discussed in quantitative terms such as LEED, BREEAM and other checklist systems that do not consider renovation potential, a building's age or its capacity for improvement. What is difficult to measure – experience, behaviour, context, architectural quality, heritage – gets ignored. There are some experimental offices that are proposing alternative approaches to green architecture, especially through architectural research in this area.[1]

Concepts in Architectural Sustainability

At the 2014 Venice Architecture Biennale, Stig L Andersson argued that experiential, architectural qualities must be paired with the rational and that each is exactly as important as the other.[2] He calls this 'complementarity'.[3] Many architects are now attempting to engage with sustainability through new language and priorities that are more humanistic and holistic. According to Simon Guy:

> We must fundamentally revise the focus and scope of the debate about sustainable architecture and reconnect issues of appropriate technological change to the social and cultural processes and practices within which a specific design is situated. Drawing upon more critical, interpretive, participative, and pragmatic approaches to sustainable design would involve researchers both in defining the nature of the environmental challenge while encouraging a wider range of context-specific responses.[4]

Guy and Steven A Moore argue that green buildings are situationally specific 'contingent hybrids'[5] inseparable from their context of sustainability, place, technology and the future.

Key concepts from *ᗡ Constructions* can be extracted to explicitly propose new ways for architects to engage with the distinctly non-architectural language of 'sustainability' through reflection upon 'the local'. Here, three examples are analysed relating to ecology, social sustainability and context-specific design that draw on the local to experimentally consider architectural qualities and connect to current trajectories in experimental green practice. Hy-Fi is a temporary pavilion that provides 1:1 testing of a completely organic building material. Complementary to this technological challenge is an intensely local one: the building's cradle-to-cradle concept largely responds to a 240-kilometre (150-mile) radius. The Liyuan Library is a small-scale community-run building that was designed as a social-architectural experiment. The award-winning project subverts expectations in terms of architectural recognition, environmental concepts and experimental building. The final example is the Great Gulf Active

House, a sustainable building prototype with the capacity to disrupt mainstream building practice due to the partnership with a commercial housing developer. This project is able to balance, not just include, architectural experience as a sustainability parameter.

An Ecological Perspective: Hy-Fi

Almost all architects now work internationally, and most projects, even intensely local ones, are supported by consultants, materials, staff, labourers and building technologies that do not come from the place where the building is located. A project that aspires to be both intensely local and scalable to a permanent building is the Hy-Fi installation by The Living. The experimental pavilion is a unique project commissioned for the Museum of Modern Art (MoMA) and MoMA PS1 Young Architects Program and installed in New York at PS1 in summer 2014.[6] Architect David Benjamin created a cathedral-like form for the 12-metre (40-foot) tall structure and partnered with

local material designers Ecovative who grew the bricks from corn stalks mixed with fungal mycelium. As part of their process, the team decided where the raw materials came from, considered what kind of energy and labour were required, imagined how the building would change over time, and planned where the building materials would go when it was deconstructed.

Benjamin saw Hy-Fi as a test bed of how architects could design for these larger ecosystems in permanent building projects. The local food movement has food miles and Benjamin wanted to start an awareness within architecture about the concept of architecture miles in terms of embodied energy and sustaining the community. The plant materials were grown in upstate New York and the building blocks are harvested agricultural waste. Then, to complete the cycle, after the building was deconstructed and composted the soil was used by Build It Green in the Queens Community Gardens. The experimental structure relates

to concepts in this Δ in that it tests unique technical and spatial possibilities while aiming to communicate a way of working beyond itself. The engineers for the project, Arup in New York, were so intrigued by it that they built another temporary structure as a party pavilion in their New York office. During the Hy-Fi installation at MoMA PS1 it was announced that software giant Autodesk was acquiring The Living for its research division.[7] Two more iterations of the brick structure are planned for 2015: an indoor application and a building scale. The focus on natural building materials and cradle-to-cradle thinking makes this an important benchmark in sustainable design and in bringing architectural and materials research into future practice.

Social Sustainability: Liyuan Library

Another influential experimental structure is the Liyuan Library by Li Xiaodong located in a village near Beijing. The library is designed as a part of the local

Li Xiaodong

Liyuan Library

Jiaojiehe, China

2012

opposite: The main space is large and bright, with integrated furniture, book stacks and steps. The library is building its collection by asking borrowers to leave two books and take one home.

above: The community-run library is located on a beautiful site and the designers aimed to draw as much from the local environment as possible. It is not connected to the village electricity grid so passive strategies are used for lighting and ventilation. The distinctive cladding is local firewood.

physical and cultural environment from the scale of material to site planning to the design of a system of book lending. Li Xiaodong aimed to use architecture to enhance appreciation of the site´s natural landscape qualities. He relates to 'sustainability' in terms of sustainable siting and local context.[8] The building has won numerous architectural awards, most recently the inaugural Moriyama RAIC International Prize of CAD$100,000, which is significant because the architect worked pro-bono on the project and the construction budget was about CAD$185,000.

The library is small, about 175 square metres (1,885 square feet), and is not connected to the local electricity grid so it uses all passive solar and ventilation strategies. The building is naturally daylit, and was inexpensive to build using local labour. At first glance, it seems to be all timber with vertical strips, but is actually glazed on the walls and roof with an exposed wood frame. The Modernist glass box is subverted by the arrangement of twigs, hand collected on site, that screen the volume. The reflecting pool in front is actually part of a passive ventilation system of operable facade elements that move air through the library, and to cool the building, the air is chilled over the pond.

When the community-run facility opened, it was empty because there was no budget for books. Opened in 2012, it has built its collection by asking visitors to donate two books for each one they borrow. The Moriyama RAIC International Prize is for a 'single, transformative work of architecture',[9] and this modest, intensely local project makes a big impact as a benchmark in social sustainability and as a demonstration that even a tiny budget can allow for a quality architectural experience.

Climate- and Context-Specific Low-Energy or No-Energy Solutions: Active House

Active Houses are a series of global sustainable demonstration projects that aim to balance energy efficiency, low environmental impact and superior indoor air quality.[10] As buildings that aim to give more than they take, they follow an approach of performance-driven sustainability and have a formal certification system. The Great Gulf Active House, the first such project in Canada, is a prototype designed by Danish designers and Toronto architects Superkül. Completed in 2013, it is located in a typical suburban subdivision, surrounded by detached, single-family homes each with similar houses and yards. This house, however, has some almost hidden sustainable features: a double-height living room that is flooded with natural light, multiple operable skylights, high-performing windows, and

Superkül

Great Gulf Active House

Thorold, Ontario

2013

The house was designed for Great Gulf, one of Canada's largest home builders, to meet the construction metrics outlined by the European Active House programme. The exterior walls, roof and floor systems were prefabricated in Toronto at Brockport Home Systems, expediting the process such that the house framing was completed in a week. Doing it this way also reduced material waste, energy use, and risks of on-site accidents during the construction process, and improved the accuracy and quality of typical suburban construction.

rainwater collection on site. The building's air and light qualities were tuned using daylight analysis simulation tools for the positioning of windows and rooflights.

Far from being imagined as a one-off, this house was built by local developer Great Gulf Group and used various industry-standard sizes, fittings and materials. The idea is not to showcase the house's technology as ideal or 'sustainable', but rather as a higher-quality product that consumers might pay more for. In the brochure it is even compared to a smartphone – consumers do not understand the technology behind it and they do not need to in order to want one. There are some clues on the outside that this is an Active House, but it does not aim to transform the suburban housing typology. It also faces somewhat inwardly, largely drawing light and air from the roof, and in some ways functions as a courtyard house with its predominantly open-plan main space.

What makes this Active House a good architecturally relevant example of localness and sustainability is its dual focus on the architectural qualities of daylight and thermal comfort, which are measured quantitatively and qualitatively, and its formal response to local environmental and social conditions, including building orientation and the suburban vernacular.[11]

Sustaining the Local

△ Constructions does not go far enough in promoting the local as a way of pushing forward an alternative approach to sustainable design. How a building's local focus addresses the lifecycle design of the building; the attitudes to community building and social sustainability; and the ways that local context can be balanced with performance criteria are some starting points for how the local can engage

progressively with the sustainable. This *△* calls for a 'productive pluralism' that allows for a multiplicity of approaches to address a design´s local specificity. A similar approach is needed for sustainable architecture. High-profile and well-published, the three examples here communicate within and beyond the profession to critique the status quo. Works such as these have the potential to contribute to a new school of thought relating to constructions that are intensely local and place-based and at the same time embrace concepts of 'complementarity' in sustainable architecture to privilege quality of experience. *△*

---

opposite right: The open-plan interior has integrated lighting and ventilation systems. A dual-zone HVAC system connected to a Somfy TaHomA Smart House system uses sensors to automate the windows, blinds and 14 skylights to open and close in response to the interior temperature and air quality. Two heat-recovery ventilation (HRV) units supply the house with fresh air.

Notes
1. Terri Peters (ed), *△ Experimental Green Strategies: Redefining Ecological Design Research*, November/December (no 6), 2011.
2. Stig L Andersson, *Empowerment of Aesthetics: Catalogue for the Danish Pavilion at the 14th International Architecture Exhibition La Biennale di Venezia 2014*, p 5: http://issuu.com/sla_architects/docs/empowerment_cover_inclusive_lowres.
3. *Ibid*, p 10.
4. Simon Guy, 'Pragmatic Ecologies: Situating Sustainable Building',
Architectural Science Review, 53, 1, 2010, p 21.
5. Simon Guy and Steven A Moore (eds), *Sustainable Architectures: Critical Explorations of Green Building Practice in Europe and North America*, Spon Press (New York), 2005, p 3.
6. Terri Peters, 'Hy-Fi', *Mark*, 56, March/April 2015.
7. 'What'a a Software Company Doing Buying an Architecture Firm?', 10 September 2014: www.forbes.com/sites/bruceupbin/2014/09/10/whats-a-software-company-doing-buying-an-architecture-
firm/.
8. Conversation with Li Xiaodong, 11 October 2014.
9. Terri Peters, 'Reporting from Toronto: Li Xiaodong Wins Inaugural Moriyama RAIC International Prize for the Liyuan Library', 13 October 2014: http://archinect.com/news/article/111179592/reporting-from-toronto-li-xiaodong-wins-inaugural-moriyama-raic-international-prize-for-the-liyuan-library.
10. Active House: http://activehouse.info.
11. Conversation with Meg Graham of Superkül, 18 November 2014.

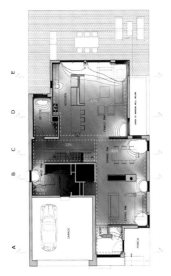

The Danish design team at VELUX used computer simulations to optimise daylighting in the home, to allow the architects to select the most efficient sizes and the most effective locations for the skylights. The architects used these to maximise direct and indirect light that is reflected off walls, ceilings and even off the engineered white hardwood strip flooring to help increase light reflectivity throughout.

CONTRIBUTORS

Barbara Elisabeth Ascher is an architect and urban planner currently pursuing her PhD at the Oslo School of Architecture and Design (AHO) where her research focuses on the design and process of architecture under conditions of scarcity and abundance. She has served as a guest-editor for the online journal *Archidoct* (Issue 1–2, 2014) and for *PLANUM* (Issue 02, 2014).

Guillem Baraut Bover graduated with honours in civil and structural engineering at the Universitat Politècnica de Catalunya (UPC) in Barcelona, and gained an MA with distinction in the Emergent Technologies and Design Programme (Emtech) at the Architectural Association (AA) in London. He is a senior engineer, partner and Board member at BAC Engineering Consultancy Group based in Barcelona. He has taught at the UPC, and is an adjunct professor at AHO in Oslo. He has received the Dragados (2003), Feidad (2006, with Mattia Gambardella) and Tsuboi awards (2013, with Defne Sunguroğlu Hensel).

Peter Buchanan worked as an architect and urban designer/ planner for a decade before joining the *Architectural Review* in 1979. Freelancing since 1992, he curated travelling exhibitions about Renzo Piano and green architecture, and has published widely in many journals. His books include the five volumes of *Renzo Piano Building Workshop: Complete Works* (Phaidon, 1993) and *Ten Shades of Green: Architecture and the Natural World* (WW Norton, 2006).

Shin Egashira makes art and architecture worldwide. Recent collaborative experiments include Time Machine (for Beyond Entropy) and Twisting Concrete, which seek to fuse old and new technologies. He has been conducting a series of landscape workshops in rural communities across the world and been teaching at the AA since 1990, where he is currently the unit master of Diploma Unit 11.

Karl Otto Ellefsen is Professor in Architecture and Urbanism at the Oslo School of Architecture and Design where he was also rector from 2000 to 2014. He is also heading the Oslo Architectural Triennial (2013) and is the President of the European Association for Architectural Education (EAAE). He is a practising architect in the field of urbanism and has produced scholarly writing on the history of urbanism and urban design, urban strategies, and architectural theory and critique. He has held different roles in the development of the policies and organisation of the Norwegian National Tourist Routes project from its inception, and is currently a member of its Board.

Lisbet Harboe is a Norwegian architect. She works at AHO in Oslo and runs a part-time architectural practice. In 2012 she completed her PhD at AHO, 'Social Concerns in Contemporary Architecture: Three European Practices and Their Works', in which she looked closely at a selection of works and strategies. She was educated at the Norwegian University of Science and Technology (NTNU) in Trondheim, and has extensive experience from architectural practice.

David Jolly Monge is an architect. He graduated from the Pontifical Catholic University of Valparaíso in Chile, and gained his PhD at UPC in Barcelona. He has been a professor at e[ad], the school of architecture and design at Valparaíso, from 1978, was Head of School from 1998 to 2003, and Dean of the faculty from 2006 to 2009. He is a founding member of the Open City in Ritoque, Chile, where he has lived since 1978. His research interests include concrete forms made with flexible formwork and the relation of architecture and poetry (Amereida).

David Leatherbarrow is Professor of Architecture at the University of Pennsylvania, where he also serves as Chairman of the Graduate Group in Architecture (PhD programme). He teaches architectural design, as well as the history and theory of architecture, gardens and cities. His recent books include: *Architecture Oriented Otherwise* (Princeton Architectural Press, 2009); *Topographical Stories: Studies in Landscape and Architecture* (University of Pennsylvania Press, 2004); and, with Mohsen Mostafavi, *Surface Architecture* (MIT Press, 2002).

Areti Markopoulou is an architect, Academic Director of the Institute for Advanced Architecture of Catalonia (IAAC) and initiator of Fab Lab Greece. As co-founder of the myCity.me non-profit organisation, her research explores how energy, information and fabrication could lead to [technology+user]-based optimum future city models that could adapt to behavioural changes over time. She is permanent faculty at IAAC and has published articles internationally. Her practice includes collaborations with offices such as R+B architects, BOPBAA, MMA Architects, Azymuth and the Barcelona Regional Agency.

Philip Nobel is the Editorial Director of SHoP Architects and the author of *Sixteen Acres: Architecture and the Outrageous Struggle for the Future of Ground Zero* (Metropolitan Books, 2005). His writing has appeared in *Artforum*, the *New York Times*, *Metropolis*, the *London Review of Books* and elsewhere.

Terri Peters is an architect and writer with a PhD in sustainable building transformation. Over the last decade she has written around 200 texts for magazines and journals on alternative approaches to sustainability, the architectural potentials of digital technologies and urban and building-scale regeneration. Currently a Post-Doctoral Fellow at the University of Toronto, she guest-edited *D Experimental Green Strategies: Redefining Architectural Design Research* (Nov/Dec 2011), co-edited *Inside Smartgeometry: Expanding the Architectural Possibilities of Computational Design* (Wiley, 2013), and co-authored the TED Studies Guide *Ecofying Cities*.

Rodrigo Rubio is an architect and faculty member at the IAAC, where he has led research projects such as the Albacete Effect, Hyperhabitat: Reprogramming the World for the 2008 Venice Architecture Biennale, the Solar Decathlon Europe FabLabHouse and the Endesa Pavilion in Barcelona. In 2005, together with Daniel Ibáñez, he founded MaRGeN, an architectural office in Madrid that focuses on landscape and self-sufficiency issues, and has received several prizes in national and international competitions.

Søren S Sørensen is an architect, educator and researcher with extensive experience from practice, tutoring and multidisciplinary research. He has published on architecture, computational design and augmented reality. He currently directs the Advanced Computational Design Laboratory (ACDL) at the Institute of Architecture at AHO in Oslo. He is a Board member and current secretary of the OCEAN Design Research Association.

Defne Sunguroğlu Hensel is an architect, interior architect, member of the OCEAN Design Research Association and the Sustainable Environment Association (SEA), and a doctoral candidate at AHO. She studied interior architecture at the Kent Institute of Art & Design in the UK, Architecture Part I at the Canterbury School of Architecture, and completed her diploma degree at the AA where she also gained her MSc in the Emtech programme. She has received the Holloway Trust, Anthony Pott Memorial, and the CERAM and IASS Tsuboi awards.

What is Architectural Design?

Founded in 1930, *Architectural Design* (ᐃ) is an influential and prestigious publication. It combines the currency and topicality of a newsstand journal with the rigour and production qualities of a book. With an almost unrivalled reputation worldwide, it is consistently at the forefront of cultural thought and design.

Each title of ᐃ is edited by an invited guest-editor, who is an international expert in the field. Renowned for being at the leading edge of design and new technologies, ᐃ also covers themes as diverse as architectural history, the environment, interior design, landscape architecture and urban design.

Provocative and inspirational, ᐃ inspires theoretical, creative and technological advances. It questions the outcome of technical innovations as well as the far-reaching social, cultural and environmental challenges that present themselves today.

For further information on ᐃ, subscriptions and purchasing single issues see:

www.architectural-design-magazine.com

Volume 84 No 2
ISBN 978 1118 452721

Volume 84 No 3
ISBN 978 1118 535486

Volume 84 No 4
ISBN 978 1118 522530

Volume 84 No 5
ISBN 978 1118 613481

Volume 84 No 6
ISBN 978 1118 663301

Volume 85 No 1
ISBN 978 1118 759066

Individual backlist issues of ᐃ are available as books for purchase at £24.99 / US$39.95

www.wiley.com

How to Subscribe
With 6 issues a year, you can subscribe to ᐃ (either print, online or through the ᐃ App for iPad)

Institutional subscription
£212 / US$398 print or online

Institutional subscription
£244 / US$457 combined print and online

Personal-rate subscription
£120 / US$189 print and iPad access

Student-rate subscription
£75 / US$117 print only

ᐃ App for iPad
6-issue subscription:
£44.99 / US$64.99
Individual issue:
£9.99 / US$13.99

To Subscribe to print or online
E: cs-journals@wiley.com

Americas
E: cs-journals@wiley.com
T: +1 781 388 8598
or +1 800 835 6770
(toll free in the USA & Canada)

Europe, Middle East and Africa
E: cs-journals@wiley.com
T: +44 (0) 1865 778315

Asia Pacific
E: cs-journals@wiley.com
T: +65 6511 8000

Japan (For Japanese speaking support)
E: cs-japan@wiley.com
T: +65 6511 8010
or 005 316 50 480
(toll-free)

Visit our Online Customer Help available in 7 languages at www.wileycustomerhelp.com/ask